SOLOMON
AMONG THE
POSTMODERNS

SOLOMON
AMONG THE
POSTMODERNS

Peter J. Leithart

Brazos Press
Grand Rapids, Michigan

Published by Brazos Press
a division of Baker Publishing Group
P.O. Box 6287, Grand Rapids, MI 49516-6287
www.brazospress.com

Printed in the United States of America

Scripture quotations are from the New American Standard Bible®, copyright © 1960, 1962, 1963, 1968, 1971, 1972, 1973, 1975, 1977, 1995 by The Lockman Foundation. Used by permission.

Library of Congress Cataloging-in-Publication Data
Leithart, Peter J.
    Solomon among the postmoderns / Peter J. Leithart.
        p.   cm.
    Includes bibliographical references and index.
    ISBN 978-1-58743-204-0 (pbk.)
    1. Bible. O.T. Ecclesiastes—Criticism, interpretation, etc. 2. Postmodernism—Religious aspects—Christianity. I. Title.
BS1475.52.L45 2007
270.8′3—dc22   2007026055

To John Arthur,
my first grandson

"Go then eat your bread in happiness,
and drink wine with a cheerful heart;
for God has already approved your works."
Ecclesiastes 9:7

Contents

Acknowledgments

This book took its earliest form as a set of lectures for the Faith and Life series at Hillsdale College in the spring of 2006, and I am grateful to Prof. Donald Westblade for the opportunity to deliver the lectures at my alma mater. I gave the same lectures in an updated form at the Dabney Center of the Auburn Avenue Presbyterian Church, Monroe, Louisiana, during the fall of 2006. Thanks to Pastor Steve Wilkins and the elders of Auburn Avenue for their hospitality and the opportunity to present this material.

A number of theologians, each far better informed than I, generously responded to some of the basic interpretations offered here. Thanks to Jamie Smith, David Hart, John Milbank, and Kevin Vanhoozer for their comments on various parts of my argument. Joel Garver read through several of my lectures, as did Berek Smith, and offered helpful corrections and criticisms.

Most of what I know of Ecclesiastes I learned from Jeff Meyers and Jim Jordan, and Jeff was kind enough to send me an advance copy of his now-published commentary, which proved very useful for organizing my own thoughts.

Thanks to Rodney Clapp, Rebecca Cooper, Lisa Ann Cockrel and the rest of the staff at Brazos Press for their interest in yet another book on postmodernism, and for their careful guidance of this project to its completion.

For several months during 2006, I was part of a postmodernism reading group that included Joshua Appel, Douglas Wilson, Nate Wilson, and occasional others. Doug and Nate were always far more suspicious of and hostile to postmodern thinkers than I, but I learned a great deal from their bracing challenges. I am sure Doug will still find things to disagree with in this little book, but it would have been a poorer book without him.

For a number of years, I have been dedicating books to my children. I've covered them all, and have considered beginning to dedicate books to my grandchildren. At the moment, this is easy enough, since I have only one, but I've been warned that, with ten children, I may well have to keep writing into the next millennium to cover the next generation. In the teeth of this sober wisdom, I have initiated a reckless trend by dedicating this book to John Arthur Leithart, my first grandchild, in hopes that he will live to see a world that is truly and thoroughly postmodern.

Peter J. Leithart
Peniel Hall
Moscow, Idaho
Second week of Lent, 2007

Introduction

Before the Beginning

When I started *Solomon among the Postmoderns*, I was aiming it mainly at anti-postmodern Christians (let's call them APCs). By presenting central postmodern themes in a way that postmodernists would recognize, I hoped to isolate the specific places where Christians must challenge postmodern theory. Many of the most vocal APCs highlight epistemological issues, challenging what they perceive as postmodern "relativism." Epistemology is not, however, as central as many APCs suggest, and at least the most sophisticated postmodern writers rarely mean to say the outlandish things APCs attribute to them (e.g., "texts can mean whatever we want them to mean"). Simon Blackburn has wisely commented that there is no "recent philosophical movement that could have been stopped in its tracks by pointing out that it is easier to find your way about in daylight than in the dark, or that if someone tells you that a bottle contains gin and you act accordingly, you have a beef against him if it contains kerosene." While admitting that some postmoderns "might have carelessly let loose remarks that seem to imply the opposite," he suggests that "they probably misspoke themselves as they tried to say something more interesting."[1] I've wanted to discover those more interesting things that postmodernists are trying to say, and as I pursued those more interesting things I increasingly found that eschatology is far more central to postmodernism, and to the Christian response to postmodernism, than epistemology.

I hoped also to show APCs that postmodernity is, in the sense that sociologists generally use the term, simply a fact. Whether we want to call it "postmodernity" or something else, and whatever we still share with the modernities of the past few centuries, we need *some* term to describe the remarkable set of interrelated cultural and political changes that marked the last decades of the twentieth century and the first decade of the twenty-first: the collapse of the bipolar political world of the cold war; the globalization of trade, finance, and business; the establishment of an American cultural and, increasingly, political empire; the renewed vigor of fundamentalist Islam in world politics, the belated discovery of the dominance of Christianity in the Southern Hemisphere, and the dissolution of denominational boundaries among post-Reformation churches; the rapid spread of new information and communication technologies; the rise of advertising, entertainment, and popular culture as *the* shared culture of the United States; new trends in immigration and urbanization; the related shifts in how theorists talk about knowledge and language, the self, and power.

One is tempted to exaggerate or to minimize the magnitude of these kinds of cultural and political shifts. We minimize these changes because change is the rule at every moment of history, and it's almost always possible to find some precedent

---

1. "Up from Bullshit," *New Republic*, October 23, 2006. Blackburn is reviewing Harry Frankfurt's *On Truth*, a sequel to his 2005 essay *On Bullshit*.

for the present in the past. We exaggerate changes because it's our life we're talking about, and we want it to be important. We need some historical balance here: though we are always living in "times of transition," some times *are* more transitional than others. We seem to be in one of those times. Some of the trends I've listed above are, I think, symptoms of an epochal shift in world history, of the kind that occurs only every few centuries. The realignment of Christian denominations, along with the southern tilt of contemporary Christianity, is among these symptoms, as is the erosion of the modern nation-state's monopoly on geopolitical clout. Other trends are pendulum swings within the modern paradigm. To respond wisely, however, Christians will have to examine more carefully what's actually taking place around us. We will want to resist some of these trends, but to resist "postmodernity" without qualification is like resisting the end of the second millennium. It's too late now, and it was going to happen anyway.

As I researched, however, it became clear that I also needed to respond to pro-postmodern Christians (let's call these PPCs), many of whom have adopted the inflated rhetoric of secular postmodernists. Convinced that postmodernism is an entirely new thing in history, without father or mother or genealogy, wholly different from the demon modernity that preceded it, PPCs encourage other Christians to shed their old-fashioned commitments to "truth" and their so-yesterday binary opposition of right and wrong and get in step with the spirit of the times. Increasingly, I have wanted not only to clarify what postmodernity is and what postmodernists are saying but also to bump some PPCs off their bandwagon.

Though each chapter includes some biblical-theological response to the issues raised, most of this book is expositional. I have aimed to make postmodern theory as plausible as possible, both by showing connections with postmodern cultural and political realities and by attempting (with what success I don't know) to describe postmodern theory at something like street level. I don't propose an "agenda" for the church in postmodern times, partly because "agendas" have a tendency to perpetuate the worst features of modern Christianity. Of course Christians must act, and act in ways that thoughtfully take account of the world in which we are acting. If "agenda" means no more than that, then I am all in favor of agendas. In that sense, St. Benedict had an "agenda" for Europe. Agendas, however, have a tendency to shortcut a thoughtful taking-account of the world and a tendency to treat Christianity as a spiritual machine. That is what I want to avoid. At times the Christian agenda may be to wait and do nothing, which, come to think of it, was a large part of Benedict's "agenda." Instead of an agenda, I propose a *stance*, a stance of faith, joy, and celebration in the midst of postmodern mist.

Beginnings

Where shall we begin? That's not an easy question. Every beginning assumes something prior. Every beginning is the beginning *of* something, and a beginning is recognizable as a beginning only because of the something that it begins.

Is a cause the beginning of an effect? We usually think so, but things are more complicated than they appear to be. Without the effect, would we recognize the cause as a cause? Does a flying baseball become the cause of a broken window before it breaks the window? It seems not. A baseball that narrowly misses a window is not a cause of breaking windows, though it may cause fear and relief in the boy who hit the ball. If the baseball becomes a cause only when it achieves an effect, which, if either, comes first? Is the cause the beginning of the effect, or the effect the beginning of the cause?

Have you ever found a pure spring, a spring with no water coming from it? Or is a spring a spring only because a stream flows from it? In itself, the beginning of a road is nothing. It is not the beginning of a road unless the beginning continues as a road.

When did your life begin? Biologically, when a sperm united with an egg. But your life would not have begun without a father to provide sperm and a mother to provide the egg. Even if your life began in a petri dish, the sperm and egg came from someone, and even if we someday figure out how to confect sperm and egg in a laboratory, there would still be scientists and scientific research before the beginning of any life. Even the beginning of a human life is not an absolute beginning.

There is always something on the far side of every beginning, beyond the beginning, which may be the real beginning. But then there is another beginning on the far side of that, and so on and on. There is also something on the near side of every beginning, and only by this is a beginning identifiable, knowable, definable as a beginning. As Solomon said, "That which is has been already, and that which will be has already been" (Eccles. 3:15). The search for beginnings is vapor and shepherding wind.

Searching for a beginning, we might soon be facing an infinite regress, or, worse, an infinite book, a Borgesian nightmare. Yet we must begin, so let's begin with my title. The title of this book is *Solomon among the Postmoderns*. Solomon I shall return to by and by. Let's begin with the postmoderns.

Immediately we are faced with questions that occur before the beginning. Before we begin, we have to consider how we are going to use the words we are going to use. *Solomon* is specific enough, but *postmodern* is used so often and so variously that it has suffered the devaluation that always follows inflation. Does it actually refer to *anything*, or is it useful only for faddish intellectuals to assert their intellectual superiority to the darkened masses? To what kind of reality, if any, does the word refer?

Clearly, *postmodern* is a generalization, and any generalization must stretch out to cover a large set of particular phenomena. Every name expresses a judgment that is a generalization. If I say a man is a "scoundrel," I mean he engages in a particular set of behaviors and displays in those behaviors a certain recurring character, the character of scoundrelhood. *Scoundrel* is a generalization, a judgment, based on my observation that he cheats at cards, flirts with women while ignoring his wife, betrays friends in matters of deepest consequence. If all those observations are accurate, the label is accurate, even if the same man takes good care of his aging mother, occasionally gives a dime to a beggar, or rubs the ears of his chocolate lab.

Unless we are going to accept the radical nominalism of Nietzsche and assign each individual leaf a proper name, we can't make do without generalizations. Even proper names, as I discuss in chapter 3, have been described as generalizations, stretching out to cover what some conceive as a sequence of quite different persons. To be *perfectly* precise, we would need to assign a new proper name to each particular thing at each passing moment. That is the way of insanity. If, as Nietzsche argues, every noun generalizes and so does violence to the unique individuality of the thing it names, it's a violence we cannot live without.[2] Generalizations simplify complex realities, but simplification is not necessarily falsehood.

2. For the record, I don't believe "violence" is a good description of what happens when we generalize or name.

When we employ generalizations about events, cultures, societies, or epochs (all themselves generalizations), the complexity of
the reality covered is far greater, and the generalization threatens
to stretch until it tears. That could be embarrassing, yet again we
cannot help risking the embarrassment. What we call the "Battle
of Actium" is a highly complex set of specific actions and reactions
by many hundreds of individuals, yet no one would want to toss
out the phrase as useless. And of course to speak of the "Roman
Empire" is to speak of something infinitely more complex than
a single battle. Generalizations are inevitable when we are dealing with historical phenomena as much as when we are dealing
with individual human beings. Given sufficient evidence, we may
speak of a "society of scoundrels" as well as of *a* scoundrel. We
may speak of a Parliament of Fools as well as of a fool. We may
speak of an epoch of incredulity as well as of an unbeliever.

One of the complexities here is that our generalizations are
among the phenomena we are attempting to generalize about.
One of the features of postmodern culture, for example, is that
many people today call our culture "postmodern." Every time
we talk about postmodernism, we contribute to the formation
and development of the reality of postmodernism, because
postmodernism is partly made up of the public discourse about
postmodernism. This is a circle, but not, I hope, a vicious one.
Like generalization, this circularity cannot be avoided.

Despite the complications, I will work on the assumption that
the terms *modernity* and *postmodernity*, *modernism* and *postmodernism*, are useful generalizations about reality.[3] To what sorts

3. Writers commonly distinguish "postmodernity," as an objectively factual social
and political condition, from "postmodernism," which usually denotes trends in theory,
philosophy, and culture. Though this distinction gets at some important factors, Mike
Featherstone has rightly noted that one of the key features of "postmodernity" as a set
of social and political facts is the intrusion of culture in economic, political, and social
life. Thus postmodernism cannot really be separated from postmodernity. When I use

of realities do they refer? *Modernity* and *postmodernity*, *modernism* and *postmodernism* refer to "cultural formations," more or less coherent sets of assumptions and beliefs, practices, institutions and structures, symbols and stories, styles of thought and behavior, leading metaphors and moods. Of course not everyone who is identifiably modern holds to exactly the same beliefs and responds to the same symbols as everyone else who is identifiably modern; not all the features of modernity are unique to modernity; and not everyone who lives in an age that is identifiably modern partakes of the mood and ethos of modernity. *Modern* and *postmodern* are, as I've said, generalizations, and do not pretend to cover every specific case. To call an age "modern" or "postmodern" is to say that certain identifiable assumptions, beliefs, practices, institutions, and styles are dominant in that age, though assessing the dominant ethos of an age incurs all the kinds of complications I have been discussing, and more. To claim, as many do, that we have moved from a "modern" to a "postmodern" culture is to say that the assumptions, beliefs, practices, institutions and styles have recently changed in significant ways.

Both components of the term *postmodern* alert us to the fact that postmodernity has a father, identified as "modernity." And that father too had a father, and that father a father, and so the genealogy stretches back to Adam. We are again faced with the challenge of beginnings, but let's bite the bullet and start with the Renaissance.[4] Let us begin, in postmodern fashion, not with a definition but with a story. Let us say, In the beginning was the Renaissance . . .

---

postmodernity, the term is meant to include the theoretical reflection usually referred to as *postmodernism*, and throughout this book I emphasize the objective social and political conditions of which postmodern theory is a part. When I talk about the theoretical side of postmodernity, I use clumsy phrases like "postmodern theory."

4. It's an ironic starting point, since the term *Renaissance*, like the term *postmodern*, includes a reference to an earlier age, but it is an irony I will embrace.

1

Vapor's Revenge

In the beginning was the Renaissance . . .

For some, the plot moves in a straight line from the Renaissance to the high modernity of the twentieth century. Medievals said the spiritual was higher than the secular, pope higher than king, and monk the highest of all. Renaissance humanists disagreed and said secular activities like farming and fighting and ruling were as important as confecting bread into body, consecrating baptismal water, or observing the liturgical hours in a darkened monastery. Inspired by pre-Christian texts and achievements, humanists criticized the institutions, assumptions, and practices of medieval church and society and imagined a different, more fully human world. Nothing human is alien to me, Seneca said, and humanists agreed. Nature, they said, has a value independent of the spiritual or supernatural world, and over the centuries since the Renaissance the natural world learned to make its own way without the help of the supernatural. The world of matter in motion became the only world, without transcendence, without mystery, without spirit. Modernity is the resulting civilization. In this story, the

19

Renaissance is not only a rebirth but a birth, the birth of the modern secular world.[1]

It is true that the Renaissance produced some features of modernity. To take one example, the Renaissance witnessed an epochal transformation of the lives, aspirations, and self-image of the European aristocracy. The cause was largely gunpowder, hailed by Francis Bacon as one of the great innovations of the age. During the Middle Ages, only highly trained and expensively equipped knights could fight. Once gunpowder made its entrance, anybody with a week's training could knock a knight from his horse from a cowardly distance. Gunpowder made old forms of warfare obsolete, and in so doing made the old formless knights obsolete, since their prestige depended on old knightly forms of warfare. Gunpowder warfare was expensive, and so were the defenses required to withstand cannonballs. Only the wealthiest lords could afford them. As a result, wealthy kings acquired a monopoly of military force, and aristocrats, eager to maintain some semblance of their earlier status, had to cozy up to the man with the guns. Aristocrats began to hang around the court, transformed from rough-hewn knights into effete "courtiers." Aristocrats didn't slink away, but they became "civilized," as an aristocracy of refinement took the place of the old military aristocracy.[2]

Tracing a direct line from the Renaissance to modernity, however, distorts as much as it illuminates. For starters, the

---

1. Francis Schaeffer popularized this story line in many books.

2. Theodore K. Rabb discusses the social effects of gunpowder warfare in *The Last Days of the Renaissance and the March to Modernity* (New York: Basic Books, 2006), 55–62. Norbert Elias describes the process by which the aristocracy became "civilized" in *The Civilizing Process*, trans. Edmund Jephcott (London: Blackwell, 2000). Though he distinguishes Renaissance from modern civilization, Rabb points to various continuities: capitalist economic life began to take form during the Renaissance, as did modern trends in urban growth and the intrusion of urban civilization into the countryside (64–67, 72).

Renaissance was not nearly as secular as often thought. Francis Bacon was a leading advocate of public support for science and of scientific investigation, and Baconism, if not Bacon himself, is often seen as a progenitor of modernity. Bacon thought humans should devote their energies to scientific investigation and technological improvement rather than morals. The reason for this, though, was largely theological. For Bacon, God's law is a revealed given and doesn't need to be discovered. Bacon's scientific investigations and technical improvements, moreover, were motivated by Christian charity; he hoped to improve the lives of people by technology. More oddly, Bacon believed he was living at the beginning of a new era of human history and that James I of England was a new Solomon who would inaugurate a regeneration (what Bacon called an "instauration" or rebuilding) of human society. Bacon was no more secular than the Renaissance mystical heretic Giordano Bruno, and in his combination of esoteric religion and scientific experiment Bacon is emblematic of Renaissance science generally.[3]

Renaissance humanists, further, did not think of themselves as "modern" in the way we do. For most of the Middle Ages and well into what we now call the early modern period, the Latin word *modernus* was used negatively. For humanists as much as for medievals, "moderns" are tiny dwarfs piggybacking on ginormous ancients. It was not until the eighteenth century that the term *modern* came to be used in its fully modern sense. In the "modern" usage of the word, to be "modern" means to break with the past, re-form the world on fresh principles, celebrate the superiority of the contemporary, act on a confident belief in inevitable and everlasting progress. By the

3. On the religious motivations of Bacon's scientific agenda, see Stephen A. Mc-Knight, *The Religious Foundations of Francis Bacon's Thought* (Columbia: University of Missouri Press, 2005).

takes on its modern meaning, science, with the
nology, had proven its ability to improve human
eenth-century intellectuals were full of hope that
reason applied as science could ameliorate the human condition
further, even if it was not quite capable of producing utopia.
Moderns believe that the ancients are infants, not giants, and
believe themselves, coming at the climax of ages of human
discovery and experience, to be the true ancients, the wisest
of history's sages. Modernity is the messianism of the contemporary, and it took form in the Enlightenment and after, not
in the Renaissance.[4]

So the story must be told differently, and told better. Let's
begin again: In the beginning was the Renaissance. (It has a
reassuring air.) The Renaissance was an era of artistic and
cultural creativity, a liberation of self, knowledge, time, space,
politics and religion, and the aftershocks of this explosive
movement reverberated for several centuries throughout
Europe.[5] Humanists challenged what they perceived as the
straitjacketed thought of medieval scholastics, emphasizing
on the one hand the boundlessness of human potential and
on the other the historically relative character of all human
culture and all human knowledge. Humanists were opposed
to systematizing, skeptical that reality could be stuffed into
one big theory. "Perspective" was a discovery of Renaissance

4. Most of the account of the origins of modernity in this paragraph is taken
from Krishan Kumar, *From Post-industrial to Post-modern Society*, 2nd ed. (London:
Blackwell, 2005), 91–99.

5. I am following the discussion of Stephen Toulmin, *Cosmopolis: The Hidden
Agenda of Modernity* (Chicago: University of Chicago Press, 1992). William Bouw-
sma tells a similar story (*The Waning of the Renaissance, 1550–1640* [New Haven,
CT: Yale University Press, 2002]), though he sees the struggle for liberation and the
imposition of order as simultaneous and contradictory impulses of the Renaissance.
Zygmunt Bauman also follows Toulmin (*Intimations of Postmodernity* [London:
Routledge, 1992], xiii–xiv).

painting, but humanists didn't let painters monopolize the idea. The Renaissance raised the epistemological challenge of the relativity of human knowledge, expressed in the Duchess's skeptical dismissal of Sancho Panza's comic vision of totality: "We do not see the whole of what we look at from one little corner."[6] Renaissance humanists bristled at the rigidity of medieval church and society, challenging the dominance of the clergy and other suffocating institutional features of medieval Christendom.

For many Renaissance humanists, the world and human existence are vapor, a whirl of change without fixity, smooth edges, or symmetry. The discovery that even the divine sun was besmirched with facial blotches and the recognition that planets did not travel in perfect circles destroyed the ancient illusion of a symmetrical heavenly world. In place of the neatly bounded universe of the Middle Ages, some humanists believed the universe might be infinite. Bruno asserted that there are "no ends, boundaries, limits or walls which can defraud us of the infinite multitude of things." Montaigne observed the swirl of fashions of thought with wry equanimity: "Before it was produced, the opposite was in vogue; and, as it was overthrown by this one, there may arise in the future a third invention that will likewise smash the second."[7] Renaissance seduction poems are *memento mori*, in which the lover reminds his beloved lady that she will soon lose the blossom of youth and rot in the grave. They are about death as much as they are about love, and the conclusion of the erotic syllogism is, Let's make love while we can, before the worms begin to try your well-preserved virginity.

6. Quoted in Giuseppe Mazzotta, *Cosmopoiesis: The Renaissance Experiment* (Toronto: University of Toronto Press, 2001).
7. Bouwsma, *Waning*, 143.

At nearly the same time that Renaissance writers were awakening to the variability, evanescence, and utter temporality
of the world, the Reformation shattered the religious unity
of Europe. Decades of horrific war followed, on a scale of
savagery Europe had not witnessed for centuries, shattering
whatever political unity had existed in medieval Christendom.
Often characterized as religious wars, these conflicts were not
simply Protestant versus Catholic battles. The real conflict had
more to do with the creation of "religion" as a circumscribed
zone of life. Emerging states carved out a separate "religious"
sphere as an arena of irrational passion that threatened social
peace, blamed religion for war, and then came riding in to save
Europe from the irrational religion they had created.[8] Regardless of how the wars are characterized, they devastated Europe.
Before Calvin died, France was at war, and in the seventeenth
century Germany's patchwork of principalities and duchies was
decimated by the Thirty Years' War (1618–48) while England
entered its "century of revolution."[9]

Everywhere, Europeans felt an apocalyptic sense of crisis.[10]
Modernity was born from this anxious trauma, in response to
a century of chaotic war. René Descartes is usually identified
as the fountainhead of modern philosophy, and his importance
lies as much in his plan to construct a self-evident, neutral basis
for intellectual consensus as in the substance of his conclusions.
Descartes admired mathematics—its clarity, the power of its
proofs, the sense that mathematics gives access to unquestioned
truth—and he aspired to formulate a philosophical method
that mimicked these features of mathematics. Mathematics

8. William Cavanaugh, *Theopolitical Imagination* (Edinburgh: T & T Clark,
2003).
9. The phrase is Christopher Hill's.
10. Rabb is particularly good on this (*Last Days*, 95–96).

and science had the virtue of being thoroughly objective. No matter what the theological convictions of the scientist or mathematician, no matter what his desires or interests, no matter what his personal predilections, if he rigorously applied the proper method, consistent outcomes would follow. Science could make Nature "speak for itself," without having to rely on fallible scientists to express it. Catholics and Protestants could both produce water by combining hydrogen and oxygen, and the fact that one affirmed a papacy and one denied it had no effect on the outcome. Similarly, Descartes wanted to show, Catholics and Protestants could both apply rigorous philosophical methods to arrive at unquestioned truth shared by all humans, whether or not they believed in transubstantiation. Method would eliminate the possibility of chance and ensure consistent outcomes. Methodological philosophy, like methodological science, was an effort to separate the inquirer from his inquiry. We can put our theological differences to the side and arrive at the same truth by following the procedures of a formal method.

The Cartesian philosophical program implied a politics, and arguably the politics came first. Religious convictions inhibited the methodological effort to arrive at truth, and therefore religious convictions had to be set aside if one wanted to discover and build on the foundations of truth. Religious conviction was, by the same token, politically disruptive. If religion was allowed to stay close to the center of public life, religious division would spawn political division, and political division would turn bloody. So long as religion played its traditional role in European Christendom, people who disagreed about transubstantiation would end up killing each other. The solution, for early modern political thinkers, was to push religious conviction to the margins of public life or into the private sphere. Modern political thought and practice, in its democratic and republican forms, represents an effort to manage religious conflict without resorting to war, and of course, totalitarian politics strive to control political life as well.

Behind the chaos of war, moderns discerned the pernicious effects of the Renaissance. Humanists acknowledged the vaporous character of human life and the world, sometimes with tragic pain, sometimes with hedonistic, but equally tragic, joy. Few Renaissance humanists believed there was much to be done about it. The world was uncontrollable vapor, and that was that. But modernity was not content to observe the chaos of the world. Living with the vapor was part of the problem. Moderns set out to tame the chaos, to shepherd the wind. Modernity was not only a response to religious war but a counter-Renaissance movement, an effort to correct the errors of Renaissance humanism and to tame and control the disordered creative energies the Renaissance had unleashed.

Against the humanist tolerance of loose ends and asymmetry, moderns made order a dominant theme of political thought and philosophy. Having lived through the disorder of the English civil wars, Thomas Hobbes was obsessed with order and argued that political order requires sovereign power to be vested in a single ruler.[11] Systems, abhorred by humanists, returned. Thomism revived in a far more rigorous form than found in Thomas himself, and Protestant theologians adopted similar methods. Methodical accumulation and systematization of data became the rule. Encyclopedias became popular. [12] Philosophy

11. Modern politics also attempted to bring method to bear on political life. Just as Descartes attempted to provide a method of philosophical inquiry that would produce true outcomes regardless of the inquirer, so modern politics attempts to erect political processes that will produce the outcomes of freedom and/or justice.

12. Bouwsma, *Waning*, 182–187.

increasingly ignored history and, like much of science, devoted itself to the study of dead things.[13]

Drama provides a useful window through which to view the differences between the sensibilities of the Renaissance and those of early modernity. Shakespeare's own plays display a thoroughly Renaissance sensibility. Cultural and intellectual boundaries are fluid and permeable. Reason and unreason are not neatly separated: Lear goes insane, but in his insanity, he suddenly sees the truth of things. Shakespeare consistently violates genre distinctions, setting comic scenes at high points in his tragedies. Gravediggers joke at Ophelia's grave at the opening of the climactic act of *Hamlet*, a "clown" (or rustic) delivers the asp to Cleopatra, and in *Macbeth* a porter with a hangover mutters about hell and his need to urinate as he goes to answer the ominous knocking on the gate of Dunsinane Castle. Shakespeare's moral outlook, if he had one, is not always easy to discern, and the outcomes are often *not* poetically just. Cordelia and Desdemona die innocently. Kings are criticized—sometimes deliberately, sometimes inadvertently—as when Fluellen praises Henry V at length by comparing him to "Alexander the Pig" (a deformation of Alexander the Big, a deformation of Alexander the Great).

English theater was suppressed during the Interregnum, and after the theater returned in 1660, Shakespeare's plays were clarified and cleaned up, purified and modernized. Boundaries between genres, classes, and categories hardened; the holes were stopped up. Nahum Tate's 1681 adaptation of *King Lear* was the dominant Lear on stage for more than a century, and it ends happily with Cordelia marrying Edgar and Lear's dynasty

---

13. This is perhaps as good a way as any to distinguish a scientist from an amateur naturalist: a naturalist is content to observe the actions and habits of living things; a scientist needs to kill and dismember in order to discover how the thing ticks.

continuing. Comic moments are expunged from tragedy: there is no Fool in Tate's *Lear*, and the *Macbeth* of William Davenant has no drunken porter. Unmetrical lines were improved, while passages that assaulted the authority of kings and the dignity of aristocrats were deleted. The messiness of Shakespeare's originals manifest Renaissance sensibilities; the clarity, order, and purity of neoclassical adaptations illustrate the instincts and goals of "modernity."

Modernity did not reach its final form all at once. Some features of modern civilization begin to take shape in the late seventeenth century but came to more complete fruition in the nineteenth and twentieth. States began to centralize during the Renaissance, and this centralization continued apace in the following centuries. It was not until the nineteenth century that Italy and Germany, for instance, became unified national polities. After the wars of religion, political thinkers argued that religion had to be kept at a distance from politics and that the state should be religiously neutral to prevent sects from competing for power. But the final separation of church and state didn't occur in Germany until Prince Otto Bismarck's Kulturkampf (c. 1871–90), and didn't come to final form in France until the period of the Third Republic (1870–1940).[14] Technological control was an aspiration of early modern scientists and philosophers but became a reality in the nineteenth century. Industrialization and urbanization, often seen as key marks of modernization, were far more pronounced in the nineteenth than in the previous two centuries. Further, modernization took shape at different times in different places. England was far more urbanized far earlier than France.

We see a similar process in modernity's efforts to control time. Premodern cultures reckoned time in "imprecise and variable"

---

14. Michael Burleigh, *Earthly Powers: The Clash of Religion and Politics in Europe, from the French Revolution to the Great War* (New York: HarperCollins, 2005).

ways, and time reckoning was closely tied to locale, so that "even in the latter part of the nineteenth century, different areas within a single state usually had different 'times,' while between the borders of states the situation was even more chaotic."[15] The rise of modernity meant the rise of uniform time, a shift impelled in part by the need to regularize transportation schedules. Mechanical clocks became widespread during the late eighteenth century, creating a uniform "empty" time, a process that reached its climax in the twentieth century, where the uniformity of time is immediately evident in the worldwide standardization of calendars and the subordination of local timekeeping to an increasingly globalized method of dating.[16] The turn from second to third millennium was celebrated throughout the world, even in cultures that have no apparent reason to date time from the incarnation of Christ. This uniformity could be achieved only by detaching time from place and by emptying time of its particular and local qualities. All of this, further, expresses the modern effort to control time, an effort betrayed by talk of "time management," "budgeting time," "saving time," and so forth. For Renaissance humanists, the temporality of life was a sign that life eluded human control. Mutability could not be checked or arrested or controlled. Moderns, by contrast, strive to be accountants and rational managers of time. As Lewis Mumford has said, "The clock, not the steam-engine, is the key-machine of the modern industrial age."[17]

Modernity promises it can bring peace among nations; it can explain everything; it can control the natural world through science and technology. As a result, humanity will free itself

15. Anthony Giddens, *The Consequences of Modernity* (Stanford, CA: Stanford University Press, 1990), 17–18.
16. Ibid., 17–18.
17. Quoted in Todd Gitlin, *Media Unlimited: How the Torrent of Images and Sounds Overwhelms Our Lives* (New York: Owl, 2003), 83.

from war, poverty, political oppression, evil, perhaps even death itself. By sculpting the vapor and shepherding the wind, modernity promises to liberate humanity from the uncertainties and imperfections that mankind has long, but wrongly, believed inherent in existence.

Us versus Them

Modernity aims to achieve its goals by erecting walls and boundaries that will keep the world neatly divided and under control. The wall of separation between religion and politics will save politics from irrational passion; the wall separating science from political interest enables science to uncover the truth of things without prejudice; impervious boundaries are erected between nature and culture, comedy and tragedy, literature and philosophy, theology and philosophy.

But the fundamental boundary is the boundary between "us" and "them."[18] That is to say, modernity is founded not only on the aspiration to control reality but on the idea of progress.

A notion of progress was inherent in the word *modern* from its earliest usage. The Latin word *modernus* was coined in the fifth century and became a popular term in Christian writing after the tenth century. From the very first, *modernus* was a term of opposition, setting apart the Christian present over against the *antiquus* of Greece and Rome. Already in its Christian usage, the term contained some of the modern meaning of modernity, since it was employed by Christians who rejected the cyclical view of time popular in the ancient world, detached human time from the cycles of nature, and professed that something new—the

18. I borrow these terms from Bruno Latour, *We Have Never Been Modern*, trans. Catherine Porter (Cambridge: Harvard University Press, 1993), though I use them in a different and much less sophisticated way than Latour does.

incarnation, death, and resurrection of Jesus—had happened in human history.[19] Christianity was the first modernity, and for Christians, those who were in the church ("us") lived in a different time from those outside ("them"). People outside the church were still living in an old world. They were behind the times; Christians were people of the future.

Modernity is both a fulfillment and a rejection of the impulses of Christianity and medieval Christendom. Christianity, after all, had promised liberation: "The truth shall set you free," Jesus himself said. And the Bible begins with God's command to Adam to "take dominion" of the lower creation, to "subdue" and "rule" it. As Christianity spread throughout Europe in the early Middle Ages, technology spread with it, often carried, surprisingly enough, by enterprising and innovative monks.[20] Modernity's belief that it is "modern" also puts a Christian concept to secular use. Moderns treat modernity as if it were a new stage of redemptive history. Like the early Christians, moderns believe that they are wholly different from those who have gone before. Like the early Christians, moderns believe that anyone who refuses to adopt modern ways in the present time is a throwback to an older world. Premoderns may be in the present, but they are living in the past and are accurately classified as "primitives," just as Christians believe that those outside of Christ are wholly "in Adam," the first man. For moderns, distinguishing "us" and "them" is thus both temporal and spatial: temporal because it distinguishes sharply between the present and the past, spatial because it distinguishes sharply between those who are up to date and those who are mired in a past that moderns have transcended.

19. Kumar, *From Post-industrial to Post-modern*, 91–99.
20. One of the best treatments is William Carroll Bark, *The Origins of the Medieval World* (Stanford, CA: Stanford University Press, 1958).

This fundamental distinction between us and them prolifer-
ates into many other distinctions. We moderns organize ourselves into rationally constituted nations; *they* are organized
by irrational blood-bound tribes. We recognize the difference
between religion and politics; they confuse the two. We separate
fine arts from daily life; with them arts and life are commingled.
We believe in equality and freedom; their lives are dominated by
hierarchy and slavery. We are rational; they are irrational. We
distinguish clearly between subjects and objects; they confuse
the two. Above all, the modern theory of progress rests on the
notion that *we* know nature as it truly is and thus have the ability
to control nature in ways *they* never imagined. We can arrive at
certain knowledge of the world through scientific investigation;
they operate by guesswork, tradition, and opinion.

The theory of progress rests on the notion that there is a cut
in time between all that went before and what comes after the
beginning of modernity. Modernity establishes itself by digging
a monumental ditch, a "great divide," between the past and
the present, between those still living in the past and those who
are fully in touch with the possibilities of the present.[21] The
modern distinction of us and them and the boundaries that
accompany it map out the world as modernity sees it. Modernity is an act of cartography, a zoning operation, an exercise
in "chrono-politics."[22]

As I will use the term, *modernity* refers to a cultural formation that has risen and become dominant in Europe and North
America and to some extent elsewhere during the last four
centuries. It is characterized by beliefs and styles of thought

21. The image of the "Great Divide" is also taken from Latour, *We Have Never
Been Modern.*
22. The term comes from Johannes Fabian, *Time and the Other* (New York:
Columbia University Press, 2002).

that aspire to reduce the complexity and evanescence of reality to stable order; it refers to the institutions that attempt to manage social, economic, religious and political, and especially religiopolitical turbulence; it refers to the scientific practices that seek to map reality in theory, often expressed in mathematical terms, and to manage and improve nature through technology; it refers to the civilization in which metaphors of "machinery" and "factory" move from the technological and economic spheres to guide political programs, architectural styles, and conceptions of the human being; it refers to the belief that human beings—at least certain human beings—despite the failures of the past, can now actually achieve this semidivine control; it refers to the culture that takes shape after a great divide has been constructed between "us" and "them." *Modernity* is the name of the social, cultural, and political apparatus that since the seventeenth and eighteenth centuries has inspired Europeans and North Americans to aspire to control vapor, to sculpt the mist, to rein in the energies unfortunately unleashed by the Renaissance and a century of religious war.

Protest Movements

Modernity has regularly faced internal opponents who challenge the modern trinity of control, progress, and freedom. Romanticism was among the earliest. Against modernity's mechanism and artifice, romanticism celebrated the natural and organic; while moderns saw progress in the ascending smoke of a factory, William Blake saw only satanic mills; while modernity celebrated the cities whose buildings sprang up like weeds, William Wordsworth sought solace in an empty landscape with a lone thatched cottage nestled among the trees; against modernity's emphasis on reason, romanticism exalted

Thoreau

intuition, imagination, and fancy; against modernity's efforts
to control, romanticism embraced the world in all its whirling
wildness. Where moderns claimed to bring rational control,
romantics felt only oppressive domination; where moderns
claimed to bring progress, romantics saw degeneration and
decay; where moderns claimed to liberate, romantics heard
fetters clanking shut on the human soul.

At the same time, romanticism accepted many of the premises
of the modernity it protested. British romantic poets initially
supported the French Revolution, the quintessential modern
political event, and George Gordon, Lord Byron fought alongside Greek nationalists; romantics saw themselves as opening
a new world of endless possibility and were deep believers in
progress, though of a different sort from modernity's; romantics were as enamored with the autonomous, transcendental,
detached ego as was Descartes, though the romantic self was a
far more sensitive and beautiful soul than Descartes' mathematician. Romanticism was in revolt against neoclassicism and
hence against antiquity (at least as interpreted by classicists),
and in this it shared characteristically modern assumptions.
Charles-Pierre Baudelaire, a French romantic, reveled in the
detritus of modern urban life, celebrating the fashionable parade
of change and presentness. But he called it *modernité*.[23]

The artistic and literary movement known as modernism—
led by poets like T. S. Eliot, novelists like James Joyce, painters
like Pablo Picasso—also protested modernity yet confusingly
shares the name of the thing it protested. Like romanticism,
modernism was schizophrenic in its criticisms of modernity.

---

23. This summarizes the account of Kumar, *From Post-industrial to Post-modern*,
109–15. Roger Lundin also points to strong continuities between Enlightenment and
romantic movements (*The Culture of Interpretation: Christian Faith and the Postmodern World* [Grand Rapids: Eerdmans, 1993]).

Modernists condemned modern urban life as infernal or, alternatively, attempted to elevate the bustle of life to artistic form; modernist architects frequently reflected the rationalism, formalism, hostility to context and locality, and mechanism that were at the core of modernity; cubist painters both critiqued modernity's rationalism and indulged modern notions of the visual.

Postmodernism is another protest movement from within modernity. Though often presented, by both advocates and detractors, as something unprecedented in the history of culture, virtually nothing about postmodernity is wholly new. If postmodernism is skepticism about dogma, there have been skeptics before—the word *skeptic* is, after all, derived from ancient Greek. If postmodernism is a carnivalesque society, the phantasmagoria of consumer culture, Disneyland writ large, entertainment culture conquering all culture, that trend started nearly as soon as there were movies and perhaps even before—Americans have always wanted to be entertained.[24] If postmodernity is the shifting parade of fashion and the search for ever new sensations and experiences, that would be nothing new to the bohemian denizens of Europe's great nineteenth-century cities. If postmodernism is tragic resignation, so was Stoicism; if it is tragic joy, so was Epicureanism; if it is the aestheticization of daily life, daily life as performance, Baldassare Castiglione's courtier would find himself well at home in the postmodern world, and so would Oscar Wilde.[25] If postmodernism unveils the fact that reality is socially constructed, it finds a precursor in the Christian thinker Giam-

24. LeRoy Ashby, *With Amusement for All: A History of American Popular Culture Since 1830* (Louisville: University of Kentucky Press, 2006).

25. Mike Feathterstone is particularly good on the roots of the postmodern mentality in nineteenth-century urban bohemianism. See *Consumer Culture and Postmodernism* (London: Sage, 1991).

who identified the "true" with the "made." If
tists employ pastiche and bricolage, assembling
ered tradition on a depthless surface, they have
in the arch*modernist* T. S. Eliot. If postmodernism recognizes the theatricality of politics, so did Shakespeare
and Machiavelli, and medieval power radiated from Christian
spectacle. If postmodern novelists break the fictional frame to
reveal and revel in the fictionality of their fictions, they are in
the venerable company of Miguel de Cervantes and Laurence
Sterne, for the European novel was deconstructed as soon as
it was constructed.

When we try to find out what makes postmodernism new, we
are again faced with the challenge of beginnings. As Solomon
said, "There is nothing new under the sun" (Eccles. 1:9).

It is far too simplistic to suggest, as some have, that the
impulses of modernity have suddenly evaporated or that postmodernity reverses every modern obsession. Postmoderns who
make these kinds of inflated claims are "surface postmoderns."
They take modernity's claims about itself at face value, without
inquiring whether modernity ever achieved what *it* claimed.
Looking at the fulfillment of the modern program in the early
twentieth century, Max Weber famously described modernization as a process of rationalization and disenchantment.
Modernity was bereft of magic and meaning, and even art was
being reduced to scientific precision and mechanism. Composers employed rational ideas of harmony, and painters like Piet
Mondrian depicted geometric shapes without feeling or depth.
Because of the progress of scientific rationality, everything was
reduced to profit-loss calculation, and the modern world that
promised freedom became an iron cage.[26] Surface postmoderns

26. David Lyon, *Postmodernity*, 2nd ed. (New Dehli: Viva, 2002), 30.

accept Weber's description of modernity as an accurate description of what modernity achieved. But it's not at all clear that the world we live in is as empty of wonder as Weber suggested.[27] I can sit at my computer in woebegone northern Idaho, not far from Fingerbone, and dash off instant communications to the corners of the world. I can barrel through the air at speeds of hundreds of miles per hour, quietly sipping coffee and reading, while hundreds of others sleep or watch movies or play cards, and within a few hours we are all on the other side of the country or the world. I can carry all the Beethoven I care to download in a machine no bigger than a cigarette case. If that doesn't fill me with wonder, what will? A deeper postmodernism will recognize that the world has never been as modernized as moderns hoped and antimoderns feared.

A deeper postmodernism also recognizes that Weber's description is itself part of a history. Nineteenth-century writers responded to industrialization, bureaucratization, urbanization, and other features of modernity with far more ambivalence and variety than Weber and other twentieth-century critics of modernity. Marx admired the achievements of the bourgeoisie even as he lamented that modernization caused all solid things to dissolve into air. By the beginning of the twentieth century, however, this ambivalence had given way to a simplistic either-or: For critics, modernity was a prison from which there was limited possibility of escape; for proponents, modernity needed only to push on ahead to achieve all the domination and freedom it promised.[28] Two-handed critics who wanted to say "yes, but" had been silenced.

---

27. Latour effectively challenges Weber's analysis (*We Have Never Been Modern*, 114–16).

28. See Marshall Berman, *All That Is Solid Melts into Air: The Experience of Modernity* (New York: Penguin, 1988).

Surface postmoderns not only take modernity's self-description at face value but continue to operate with a modern notion of progress. They accept the fundamental distinction between "us" and "them." Modernity assumes that everything in the present modern moment is, or should be, purely modern, novel, sleekly now. Anything that is not up to date is an "archaism" that needs to get with the program or face elimination. Moderns worry constantly that this trend or that event might "turn back the clock." Surface postmoderns remain within the framework of modern temporality, and precisely at those points where they are most critical of modernity. For surface postmoderns, postmodern styles and moods are cutting edge, and anything sincere, unironic, passionate for truth is a throwback to dreaded "modernity." Postmodern theologians who accuse other theologians who insist on some form of epistemological realism of being "old-fashioned modernists" are being perfectly modern even as they preen themselves postmodernly, since they assume that the present moment is, or ought to be, a purely postmodern, constructivist moment. Postmodern cultural critics (mainly Christians—secular sociologists are rarely so simplistic) who assume that everything in U.S. culture changed thoroughly, permanently, and irreversibly sometime in the last two decades are also still operating in an entirely "modern" framework.

In its most interesting forms, postmodernity challenges the fundamental distinction of "us" and "them," recognizing that modernity has never been what it has claimed or aspired to be. This deeper postmodernity recognizes the fractures in the modern edifice and also recognizes that postmodernity is a result of a complex set of processes within modernity. The ways in which deeper postmodernity challenges the building blocks of modernity are varied. Postmodernity brings changes of style and mood, and it also brings important structural shifts in politics, culture, economics, and society. But these stylistic and structural changes often rise from the effects of modernity itself. Some features of postmodernity are *intensifications* of modernity; some intensifications of modernity have produced *inversions* of modernity, where modern impulses and agendas go so far in one direction that they turn into something quite different, even opposite. Some of the inversions of modernity are the result of *unmaskings*, in which the events of recent decades belie modern aspirations, or postmodern theorists claim to discern the real truth behind the modern pretense about us and them or modernity's promises of domination and emancipation.

Intensification, inversion, and unmasking are not entirely discrete cultural trends. They overlap and interpenetrate in complex ways. When Michel Foucault, for instance, unmasks modern liberal states as mechanisms of domination and power, he is intensifying the critique of institutions that began with the Enlightenment to the point where the critique turns on the Enlightenment project itself (an inversion).[29] Yet these three maneuvers help to isolate the differences between modernity and postmodernity and how we got from one to the other.

The intensifications, inversions, and unmaskings all lead in a similar direction. Modernity is the civilization that attempted, with quite astonishing successes but also blatant failures, to manage and shepherd the vapor of time, society, and nature. Postmodernity is vapor's revenge, the recognition of modernity's failures and an embrace of the fragmentation and dissolution of politics, selves, language, life.

---

29. Thanks to S. Joel Garver of LaSalle University, personal communication, November 9, 2006, for this way of formulating the relationship.

Intensifications

In many respects, contemporary culture continues and exaggerates modernity's dream of control, progress, and liberation. Scientific aspirations may be under attack from philosophers, but most scientists seem hardly to notice. Efforts to map the genome and manipulate the genetic code are thoroughly modern efforts to eliminate chance and control nature. We are told that we will very soon be able to order a designer baby, genetically constructed to our specifications. There is no "post" in this modernity at all; this is modernity is in purest, rawest, most inhuman expression. Enormous amounts of money and energy continue to be poured into technological improvements, and to the modern increase in speed of travel and communication postmodernity adds a hyperactive increase in the movement of images.[30]

Consumerism is often cited as a particular feature of postmodern life, but today's consumerist drive intensifies economic trends that have been at work for the past century. In consumer culture, people gain their identity and significance through what they purchase and own, but owning a house with a yard, two cars, a dog, and a television has been the American dream since the early decades of the twentieth century—decades that hardly meet the description of "postmodern."[31] Consumer choices are greatly expanded today. We can choose from scores of breakfast cereals, hundreds of channels, millions of websites. Yet consumer choice has been a feature of modernity from the beginning. As Zygmunt Bauman says, traditional communities are rivers, while modern societies are oceans. A river

30. Gitlin, *Media Unlimited*, 71–117.
31. See, for instance, Lendol Calder, *Financing the American Dream: A Cultural History of Consumer Credit* (Princeton, NJ: Princeton University Press, 1999).

has a direction and carries you along with the current, just as traditional societies direct their members in a particular way. In modern societies there is no current; we can choose to go any direction, no direction, or to shift direction with every change of winds.[32]

Contemporary writers often claim that the world has sped up and is now careening out of control. The sense of rapid movement, of disorientation and vertigo, the liquid feeling that nothing stays put, is partly a product of the dominance of media. Especially in urban areas, we are bombarded by messages and rapidly changing images, and these messages and images press themselves on us through advertisements, television, computers, video games, overstuffed magazine racks at the local Barnes & Noble. Novelty is put at a premium, as it always has been in the modern world, but we are more aware of novelty than ever before. One of the main speedups of the last century has been an increase in the distribution rate of new technologies. After the telephone was invented, "it took sixty-five years to reach 75 percent of American households," while televisions spread to 75 percent of American homes within only seven years.[33] Given the pervasiveness of media and advertising, changes in clothing fashion are instantly known, and the half-life of celebrity becomes ever shorter. For many, life takes place in the context of these rapidly changing images and messages, and this produces a deep sense of the vaporousness of reality.[34] In an important sense, this expresses the modern aspiration to control, for super-fast images represent one method of overcoming (or gnostically denying) time. Friedrich Nietzsche and George

32. Zygmunt Bauman, *Liquid Life* (Cambridge: Polity, 2005).
33. Gitlin, *Media Unlimited*, 85.
34. This is the genuine insight in the rhetorically overblown work of Jean Baudrillard.

Eliot complained that things moved too rapidly, and they were writing in the nineteenth century.[35] Like many modern advances, the domination of time turns into its opposite; absolute control of time through absolute speed, speed for its own sake, leaves us feeling we have no control of time.

Modernity has always suffered from basic internal contradictions. On the one hand, it aspires to control the cosmos; on the other hand, it is driven by a critical spirit that ultimately dissolves all traditions.[36] On the one hand, it is a movement of rationalization, yet on the other hand, wherever modernity spreads it is a solvent of traditional stabilities, precisely because it subjects the traditional patterns of life to rational critique and revision and seeks to overcome the inefficiencies of traditional ways. Unquestioned authorities are questioned, tribes change "how we've always done things," individuals are liberated to make choices that have never been available before. Modernity imposes on traditional societies the "heretical imperative,"[37] the demand for choice. McDonald's challenges local foods, and presents the hitherto unknown choice between maize and a Big Mac; Africans are as likely to be wearing jeans as traditional dress; communications technologies open once-isolated tribes to cultural possibilities they had never conceived of. A missionary friend tells me that members of the tribe where he ministers own cell phones but have never seen a flush toilet. The corrosive effects of modernity are found already by Marx's 1848 lament "all that's solid melts into air." One way to describe postmodernism is that modernity's solvents have been turned on modernity itself, and modernity, wolflike, eats up itself.[38]

35. Gitlin, *Media Unlimited*, 73.
36. Mike Featherstone, *Undoing Culture* (London: Sage, 1995), 150.
37. The phrase is Peter Berger's.
38. This from Lyon, *Postmodernity*. Bauman also describes postmodernism as the self-dissolution of modernity: once modernity becomes a tradition, the modern

Economically, many have suggested that we have entered a "postindustrial" age, an information economy, where producers of symbolic goods make up a larger proportion of the economic life than ever and service industries are growing rapidly. Yet in many ways, we are still in a perfectly modern economy. Heavy, roaring, sputtering, gas-fueled machinery is still being built and used, cars and trucks cannot be produced without tons of grease and oil and power tools, and Ford's Toronto plant produces fifteen hundred Windstar minivans a day. There are more cars and trucks on the roads today than ever, moving faster than ever. Computers were once thought capable of producing a paperless society, but in most cases computer use vastly increases paper use and vastly increases the tonnage of waste paper. We have not entered the postindustrial or information economy that some predicted.[39] Globalization, further, did not begin in the 1980s but, in its current form, has been going on at least since the age of exploration. Pepper became a staple in Europe and the United States because of international trade during the modern age.

Inversion

Yet the last part of the twentieth century did witness economic changes of significant magnitude, sometimes reversing the economic trends of modernity precisely by pressing those

---

critique of tradition turns on modernity itself, dissolving and destroying until it has nothing left to critique and loses its zest (*Intimations of Postmodernity*, viii). Many scholars emphasize the resistance of traditional cultures to modernity. The flow of influence is not unidirectional.

39. Much of the information here is taken from John Thackara, *In the Bubble: Designing in a Complex World* (Cambridge, MA: MIT Press, 2006). Lyon suggests that postmodernism is in part the disillusionment following the collapse of the promise of postindustrial information society (*Postmodernity*, 53–54).

trends to extremes. Two of the characteristic organizational forms of modernity—the factory system and the nation-state—have morphed in ways made possible by the technological progress of modernity.

From the pin factories of Adam Smith to the Ford assembly lines of the early twentieth century, the centralized factory has been a chief institution and symbol of modern capitalism. Few economic institutions characterize modern life more than the factory, spewing smoke in a Dickensian cityscape. But the centralized factory is not nearly as central as it was before. Centralized corporations are hardly a thing of the past, but many corporations have their operations spread to the four winds. Components of a manufacturer's final product are often made on several different continents, and assembled on yet another. Factories, many of them gigantic, still exist, but the factory system is dissipating into a network of smaller concerns. Small firms contract with larger firms and because of their smaller size have the flexibility to adjust rapidly to consumer demands. Together, the smaller companies sometimes form a "roofless factory." Communications technologies were critical to the expansion of modern economic life in the early twentieth century, but the speed and flexibility of communications has dramatically increased in just a few decades, and this has made new forms of industrial production possible. Several of my friends in small-town northern Idaho, where I live, work with high-tech firms whose central offices are several states away. Air transportation has increased in speed and convenience, becoming a major tool of international trade.

Corporations today experiment with flexible scheduling, an ever-changing pool of employees, and flexible work locations and hours. Instead of setting up a career track that will carry an employee through age sixty-five, corporations hire employees for projects that have a built-in terminus. Instead of a career, most workers will be employed for a series of more or less connected "jobs."[40] Instead of a pyramidal flow chart, companies are organized as a web, spread out on a grid of computer terminals. The flow of information moves from manager to worker and back, and workers are electronically monitored with even closer surveillance than on a factory floor.[41]

Instead of steel and coal, many of the most influential and wealthy corporations today deal in soft goods, cultural goods, and services—producing software, TV shows, or films rather than cars and trucks. The new elites are not only managers, engineers, or theorists operating within traditional modern disciplinary boundaries, but television writers and producers, screenwriters, software engineers, theorists whose work ignores disciplinary boundaries, advertising executives. Entertainment has become one of America's main exports, and Los Angeles, often cited as *the* postmodern city, has systematically (though selectively) deindustrialized.[42]

Over the past several centuries, national boundaries—and geography more generally—have been one of the defining realities of the nation-state. But those boundaries have begun to dissolve, precisely because modern technology has been so successful. Geography means less than it used to. Floating free of any physical commodity—including paper—currencies now cross borders with electric speed, and in some places national currencies are being replaced either with regional currencies (the euro) or with stronger currencies of neighboring countries (the

40. David Lyon, *Jesus in Disneyland: Religion in Postmodern Times* (Cambridge: Polity, 2000), 89.
41. Lyon, *Postmodernity*, 52.
42. Ibid., 75.

dollar in some Latin American countries).[43] National cultures haven't disappeared, but due to progress in communications and transportation, national cultures have spilled beyond national boundaries. You can eat Chinese food even in small-town America, and KFC has become the largest fast food chain in China, opening a couple hundred stores a year and planning to open Taco Bells. Hybrid cultures are everywhere: At P. F. Chang's Chinese Bistro in Vegas you can get something called "Chinese tacos," and texascook.com provides a free recipe for Texmex egg rolls.

Global corporations are increasingly common, and not all global corporations are big. Many are unbelievably huge, with Microsoft, Wal-Mart, Lucent, and others being richer than many countries. But smallish firms are also increasingly international. A town over from my home in little Pullman, Washington, is an energetic but comparatively small engineering firm, Schweitzer Engineering Laboratories (SEL), which sells its digital monitoring and control technologies for power systems in about a hundred countries. SEL employs thirteen hundred people, has opened thirty-five domestic offices, operates in twenty-four locations internationally, and has support teams or sales reps in Australia, Bahrain, Bolivia, Brazil, Canada, China, India, Italy, Mexico, Netherlands, New Zealand, Peru, South Africa, and the United Kingdom.[44] American business is no longer confined to America—something inconceivable without modernity's technological gains.

A different sort of inversion produces postmodern skepticism about modern conceptual and technical control. Quantum

---

43. Walter Truett Anderson, *All Connected Now: Life in the First Global Civilization* (Boulder, CO: Westview, 2001), 58–61.

44. Thanks to my friend SEL programmer Max Ryan for providing this information.

mechanics discovered what appears to be a degree of irreducible uncertainty in the fundamental structures of physical reality, and Kurt Gödel's "incompleteness theorem" challenged foundation-alisms with the claim that every formal system of mathematics contains an undecidable formula and that a system's consistency cannot be proved within the system. Though Sigmund Freud was a worshiper of science, his discovery of unconscious drives and motivations undermined the scientific ideal of objectivity. As Ernest Jones, an early Freudian, argued, "We are beginning to see man not as the smooth, self-acting agent he pretends to be, but as he really is, a creature only dimly conscious of the various influences that mould his thought and action, and blindly resisting with all the means at his command the forces that are making for a higher and fuller consciousness."[45] Freud's tragic sociology was an assault on Marxist or other modern dreams of a utopian future. Modern man is known and con-trollable; Freudian man is not.

Postmodernism has been characterized as an assault on the social and cultural boundaries erected by modernity.[46] One of the key boundaries of modernity was that between indus-try and culture. A cabinet may be aesthetically pleasing, but because it's functional it doesn't qualify as high art. Modern art institutions—museums, critics, art schools—conspired to ensure that art remained distinct from everyday life. Art was for the salon or the museum, the university or the playhouse, but when you needed to get from Austin to Dallas or send a message back from Dallas to Austin, what you wanted was

45. Ernest Jones, *Hamlet and Oedipus* (New York: W. W. Norton, 1976).
46. John Milbank, *Being Reconciled: Ontology and Pardon* (London: Routledge, 2003). Milbank suggests that the boundary-transgressing mania of postmodernity is an exaggeration of an original Christian impulse. The gospel, after all, announces the end of boundaries of clean-unclean and holy-profane that had dominated Israelite and pagan religions for millennia.

speed, reliability, precision, and the packaging be damned. Some within modernity—romantics and modernists especially—challenged this dissociation of sensibility, believing that art could and should have a redemptive effect on the rest of life. Many moderns, however, thought art pointless or nonsensical or at least irrelevant to the needs of daily life, and the separation between art and the rest of life was assumed by nearly everyone, even many artists.

Modernist artists and movements challenged this segmentation: Marcel Duchamp placed a urinal on a wall and got it exhibited in a museum, and Andy Warhol spent his life painting soup cans and movie stars. These artists were the harbingers of the postmodern aesthetic mood. At the same time, like the bohemian movements of the early twentieth century, postmoderns attempt to turn life into an artistic project. The wall of separation between art and life has become permeable in both directions, as everyday objects are treated as art objects and as aesthetic motivations and themes infiltrate everyday life. A key feature of the postmodern ethos is thus the "aestheticization of everyday life."[47]

Today, commerce has become thoroughly infused with cultural values, with aesthetics. Ford's Model T—available in any color, so long as it was black—is the paradigmatic modern product: made for efficiency and utility rather than beauty. Consumers went along, looking for the best buy to serve their transportation needs. Today, cars are built and marketed for the pleasure they bring to the buyer: the pleasure of driving while listening to Vivaldi—always Vivaldi, or Pachelbel—coming from a surround-sound speaker system; the pleasure of watching neighbors stare in envy at the sleek lines and bright

47. The phrase is used by Featherstone.

colors; the pleasure of extra gadgets and knobs and dials and readouts that have very little to do with transportation. If you doubt the intrusion of aesthetics and cultural concerns into the mundane, you might want to check out the prices on the designer toilet brushes at Target.[48] I've often said, reflecting on my eldest daughter's taste in cars, that a car is not a mode of transportation but a fashion accessory. Perhaps it always has been for young women, and for young men; but what is fresh in postmodernism is that the automobile industry agrees and has the flexibility to adjust to changing tastes. In short, one of the key boundaries of modernity—that between culture and economy—is dissolved, as more and more industry becomes culture industry—the Disneyfication of economic life.

As the boundaries between aesthetic and functional have been challenged, cultural products have become commodities, subject to the economic forces of supply and demand. This is partly an effect of easy reproduction. Paintings can be downloaded from the web, and we can play symphonies at will on various musical devices. But *culture* here also refers to values, aspirations, dreams, and goals, which are now manipulated and employed by companies seeking to sell lifestyles as well as products. Advertisements don't sell goods; they lend lifestyle value to goods, and what they really sell is happiness.

Once the boundary between art and life is breached, the hierarchy of high and popular culture soon collapses. Modernists like Eliot once fondly hoped that poetry would trickle

48. On this, see David Brooks, *Bobos in Paradise: The New Upper Classes and How They Got There* (New York: Simon and Schuster, 2000); Virginia Postrel, *The Substance of Style: How the Rise of Aesthetic Value Is Remaking Commerce, Culture, and Consciousness* (New York: Harper, 2004). Brooks's book focuses on a particular class and raises the possibility that postmodernism is largely class specific. These just happen to be the most articulate classes around, the talking classes that shape our perceptions about contemporary life.

down from Parnassus to refresh the language of the common
people, but the language of postmodern commoners is taken
from advertising jingles, TV shows and movies, pop music,
and news sound bites. Our cultural literacy is not gathered
from snippets of Western classics but from ever new surges of
popular culture. Treatment of Shakespeare, as always, provides
a barometer of cultural trends. On the one hand, the Royal
Shakespeare Company advertises *Coriolanus* with a poster
that invokes the film *Natural Born Killers*; serious Shakespeare
adapts itself to popular culture. On the other hand, Disney's
The Lion King retells the story of *Hamlet*—regicide, unscrupu-
lous uncle, temporizing prince, the whole thing—but ensures a
happy ending for Simba and his quite sane Ophelia.[49]

The modern academy and modern research have characteristically preserved disciplinary boundaries. At a modern university, different faculties employed different methods of analysis
and research to study history, literature, sociology, economics,
political science, biology, psychology, physics, chemistry, engineering, and so on. That life is not so neatly organized was not
lost on modern academics, but for heuristic purposes everyone
behaved himself and stayed in his cubicle. A historian left the
analysis of literary works to the literature professors, few of
whom would be so bold as to comment on Marx's critique of
capitalism. All that has changed, and many of the most active
sectors of academic life are devoted to "theory," an amorphous
cross-disciplinary nondiscipline whose practitioners mingle
Freud and Marx and social history and references to pop music
in a treatment of Chaucer or Gauguin. In the midst of this
restructuring of the academy, theology has made a comeback.
French philosophers are today as apt to wrestle with Augustine

49. Douglas Lanier, *Shakespeare and Modern Popular Culture*, Oxford Shakespeare
Topics (Oxford: Oxford University Press, 2002), 48, 85–86.

or Aquinas as with Kant and Heidegger. Modernist boundaries are dissolving, and the vapor has its revenge.

The rise of cultural anthropology has been one of the key driving forces in the development of postmodernity, insofar as it challenges modern assumptions about us and them. Cultural anthropology is an invention of the nineteenth century and was motivated by the desire to study other cultures "scientifically." Yet this scientific effort has turned on itself, in two ways. On the one hand, cultural anthropology has become a cross-disciplinary field, influencing the way ancient and medieval historians, sociologists and political scientists, students of religion and philosophers of science go about their business. Everyone talks about "culture" these days, and they learned to talk about culture from anthropologists. Cultural anthropology is thus partly responsible for the dissolution of disciplinary boundaries in contemporary universities. On the other hand, cultural anthropology has exponentially increased our exposure to alternative cultural forms and hinted at the relativity of modern Western ways. Cultural anthropologists have a habit of suggesting that *we* are not nearly so advanced, rational, and scientific as we pretend to be.

Ecclesiastically, the modern church—that is, the church since the post-Reformation wars—has been divided into various traditions and denominations. In the West, the great divide is between Catholicism and Protestantism, and the latter has subdivided into an ever-proliferating diversity, such that many non-Catholic churches (charismatic congregations, Bible churches, and others) share relatively little with mainstream Reformers like Luther and Calvin. For many centuries, one of the main jobs of theologians was to ensure that their particular tradition remained uninfected by rivals. Lutheran theologians devoted themselves to being not-Calvinists, and all Protestants were busy being not-

Catholics. Today, though, denominational boundaries are dissolving.[50] This arises partly from disgust with the fragmentation
of Christianity and the growing sense that this, just possibly, was
not what Jesus intended when he prayed that "they may all be
one" (John 17:21). But grassroots ecumenical activism has also
had its effects. Catholics have stood shoulder to shoulder with
Protestants in prolife marches, and both have discovered how
much they share. Evangelical Protestants, traditionally the lowest
of the Low Church, are rediscovering the riches of the patristic
and medieval traditions, while Vatican II and the charismatic
movement have altered the feel and order of the Catholic Mass.
For the past several centuries, the Christian world was roughly
divided between the Christian world that sent missionaries (Europe and the United States) and the "dark continents" waiting for
the light of the gospel.[51] In what is perhaps the most surprising
development of recent times, missionary and mission field have
begun to change places, as Africans send missionaries to evange-
lize secularized Europeans and Americans. This is a major shift
in church history but also a remarkable inversion of cultural
history—*we* are suddenly learning Christian faith from *them*!

These ecclesiastical inversions of modern church order are the
most important feature of postmodernity and the most potent
signs that postmodernity is something more than a passing fad.
These are changes of world-historical significance.

Unmaskings

Technical failures contribute to postmodern unmasking.
Early in the nineteenth century, Germany undertook one of

50. Lyon, *Jesus in Disneyland*, 94.
51. Ibid., 104.

the most ambitious civil engineering projects ever attempted in central Europe—the "rectification" of the Rhine River in an effort to prevent flooding along the Rhine Valley and "to create a faster, deeper, shorter river whose formerly marshy plain could be turned over to agriculture." This was only one of many water management projects that played a role in the creation of modern Germany—draining the floodplains of the Oder River, redirecting the Upper Rhine, monumental dam projects. It is an archetypal modern plan involving the management of the one of the most unmanageable of natural substances, water. It was a massive project to shepherd the wind and sculpt the mist. Despite many successes, floods continue to occur, though recent floods along the Oder have devastated portions of Poland and the Czech Republic rather than Germany—perhaps that was the plan all along.[52]

The German water management project stands as a parable of modernity, and of postmodern disillusionment with modernity's efforts to control the world. Moderns tried to instill shock and awe through smoke, pumping pistons, a loud voice; postmoderns pull back the curtain to find a little old man running the show, and not all that effectively.[53] Postmodernism arises in part from the recognition that technology has never achieved the control it promised and claimed, that science—marked as it is by debate, uncertainty, contested evidence—has never been as unified and stable as the textbooks make it appear.[54]

---

52. The full story is told by David Blackbourn in *The Conquest of Nature: Water, Landscape, and the Making of Modern Germany* (New York: W. W. Norton, 2006). I am relying on the review by Christopher Clark in the *Times Literary Supplement*, September 8, 2006.

53. For the Oz reference, see Walter Truett Anderson, *Reality Isn't What It Used to Be* (San Francisco: HarperSanFrancisco, 1990), chap. 2.

54. Latour, *We Have Never Been Modern.*

Unmaskings also take place in cultural styles, as artists and writers unmask modern claims of universalization by showing that what Westerners call "universal" truths and styles are a veiled form of Western domination. Modernist architecture is one of the most dramatic expressions of modern styles and aspirations. Modernist buildings are machinelike, factorylike, even when they're not factories or machines. Modernist architects thrive on solving formal problems and are indifferent to the uses to which a building will be put or the social, cultural, or physical location of the building. A curtain of steel and glass will work just as well for apartments as for offices and will fit as easily in Bogotá as in Boston. The universalist aspirations of modernity—that modern scientific and technological culture can provide a universal language and culture—are neatly expressed in modernist architecture. Modernist architecture embodies the distinction of us and them in glass and steel: Modernist architecture says, "We are the world." Modernist architecture says, "We have no past; there is nothing not-modern about our buildings or about us."

Postmodernism contests this universalist pretension. Postmodern architecture takes many forms, but one of its recurring interests is to speak a local language. Postmodern architects want government buildings to look like government buildings, homes to look like homes, Spanish buildings to look Spanish. In place of the universal, austerely formal language of modern architecture, they employ ornamentation, often drawing ironically from a variety of architectural periods and styles, deliberately blurring the modernist contrast of present-us and past-them. The faces of their buildings are not geometrically organized but organically various. Though "only" a change of fashion, the development of postmodern architecture marks an important movement from modern to postmodern sensibilities and arises from skepticism about the universa modernity.

Conclusion

Postmodernity is, in sum, a knot of cultural, philosophical, and social developments, arising from intensifications, inversions, and unmaskings of modernity, which challenges, doubts, and rejects the modern trinity of control, liberation, and progress. Postmodernity contests modernity's aspiration to sculpt the mutable mist of the world. Postmodernity is vapor's revenge.

This description of postmodernity and postmodern theory is, I hope to show, evident in my specific areas of interest—language, the self, and power.[55] But the most compelling signal comes not from the theories that postmodern writers construct but from the materials they use to construct them. Postmodernity betrays itself as an embrace of vapor not by its theories so much as by its tropes, not by its methods so much as by its metaphors. Modernity's master metaphors were mechanical and scientific: Newton's mechanistic universe runs by laws expressible in mathematical terms; politics was reduced to a science, and then so was the study of the human soul; repetition marked much modern architecture, so that buildings resembled machines and homes often looked like factories. "Works like

55. Even here the differences of postmodernism and modernity are not absolute. Postmoderns emphasize the limitations and fragility of reason and language, but Hume was deeply interested in the role of passions in human thought and experience, and Francis Bacon already recognized the effect that passions have on scientific inquiry. Postmodernism is also continuous with modernity in its emphasis on critique. Critique of traditional structures and ideas was more fundamental to the Enlightenment ethos than was the basis of critique itself. Some Enlightenment figures were rationalists, but many were more pragmatic and empirically oriented. What they shared was the belief that tradition should be subjected to rational critique, however that rationality was conceived.

clockwork" was an expression of success. Postmoderns are apt to use organic metaphors, but even more to use metaphors of disintegration, metaphors of dissolution, flexibility, fluidity, liquidity, fragmentation, dissemination, dispersion.[56] For postmoderns, human knowledge is always partial, provisional, fragmentary, indeterminate, tentative. Postmoderns feel themselves, and their world, melting, thawing, resolving into a dew.

So here is the storyline I suggest: The Renaissance saw that life was vapor, and it either rejoiced or despaired, but in the main considered vapor to be an unavoidable feature of human existence. Renaissance humanists had a high tolerance for uncertainty, probable knowledge, political tumult, social mobility. Following the Reformation, however, Europe was decimated by a century of war. Modernity began not from the Renaissance but in the wake of religious war, and modern thinkers, politicians, and scientists set out on a centuries-long project of controlling the vapor and roil of the world, so as to ensure that the world would never again be thrown into the tumult of what they described as religious conflict. Modernity's control has been so effective that some believed it had been achieved, until mist leaked out under the laboratory door. As an economic and social system, postmodernity is a historical demonstration that modernity's control was illusory in important respects, and postmodern theory is the intellectual reflection on this historical demonstration.

So: Modernity builds a glass and steel office box-building, a housing project that looks like and is intended to be a "machine for living"; postmodernity's buildings are ironically decorated with symbols from a half-dozen architectural styles. Modernity zones the city into commercial, residential, educational, and

56. See the list of book titles in Featherstone, *Undoing*, 1.

other areas; postmodernity integrates life, work, and leisure in a local neighborhood. Modernity mechanizes the universe and the human person; postmodernity disperses the self and the universe in a fluid organism. Modernity is a Newtonian universe, a machine operating by mathematically expressible laws; postmodernity is an expanding universe, which is perhaps alive, and postmoderns are convinced that scientific laws are less discovered than invented. Modernity says bigger is better; postmodernity says, Not necessarily, and Who says? Modernity unifies diverse groups into a nation-state, an ethnically and culturally homogenous national community, organized by a central bureaucracy, perpetuated by universal public education; postmodernity diffuses into a multiethnic nation that threatens to fragment into a loose confederation. Modernity drums out regular rhythm, like a piston; postmodernity is syncopated. Modernity manages the economy, whether through a centralized party bureaucracy or through a central bank's manipulation of credit; postmodernity thrives on a flexible global economy that escapes the management and control of any single government. Modernity reduces the world to hard particles; postmodernity reduces the particles until matter dissolves into energy. Modernity tracks GNP, GDP, and the trade deficit, convinced that a change in policy can improve them; postmodernity is more interested in quality of life and sustainable growth, with attention to the ecological impact of economic activity. Modernity marches; postmodernity flows. Modernity is statistical analysis; postmodernity is outcomes-based and qualitative. Modernity shops for goods in a one-stop department store; postmodernity shops for pleasure in a megamall of specialty shops. Modernity systematizes theology and declares popes infallible; postmodernity says theology is more like poetry, turns the priest around to face the congregation, and gives him a banjo. Modernity

neatly divides human life into zones of activity and interest—
separating home and workplace, work and leisure, business
and high culture, religion and politics; postmodernity breaches
those boundaries by returning work to the home, by making work fun, by selling elegantly styled cultural products, by
mixing religion and politics, by displaying a urinal in an art
museum. Modernity gets down to business, testing hypotheses
with well-designed experiments and diligent library research;
postmodernity frets aloud about whether research is even possible, grumbles about the difficulties of knowing anything about
the world or the past, and hedges all conclusions with a fifty-
page theoretical introduction to every book. Modernity hopes
that high culture will seep down and raise the stinking masses
from their slough; postmodernity destroys the boundaries of
highbrow and lowbrow and swallows everything up in a mass
of commercialized pop culture. Modernity wears a suit to the
office and slippers at home; postmodernity works at home in
a bathrobe and wears jeans to the office. Modernity is a city
under smog, its buildings blackened by factory smoke; postmodernity is the green belt around London. Modernity is a clock;
postmodernity is a turbulent stream, a swiftly moving weather
system. Modernity is checkerboard; postmodernity is fractal.

In a word, modernity is mid-twentieth-century Detroit; postmodernity is Vegas.

2

The Elusive Word

Postmodern relativism—it rolls tripplingly off the tongue, and for many APCs relativism is the most defining, and the most threatening, feature of postmodernism. For the relativist, all beliefs are equally valid, all moral judgments equally correct, all aesthetic determinations equally founded—or unfounded, as the case may be. Relativism is embodied in many of the popular slogans and attitudes of the past century: "anything goes," "to each his own," "beauty is in the eye of the beholder," "have it your way," "I did it my way." Relativism embraces difference and diversity for its own sake and considers all efforts to organize or limit diversity to be misguided at best, fascist at worst.[1]

1. In fact—and it's a subtle point—if everything is simply different from everything else, then differences are all the same. For the relativist, a walnut is different from a candlestick in the same way and to the same degree that a buffalo nickel is different from a quasar. But if we can't distinguish different sorts and degrees of difference (which is the same thing as distinguishing sorts and degrees of similarity), then saying everything is the same makes as much sense as saying everything is different. So it is that the extreme celebrant of difference joins hands with the celebrant of sameness, the absolute pluralist is blood-brother to the absolute monist.

In most of its forms, relativism is obviously self-refuting. If all beliefs are equally valid, then the fundamentalist's belief that all beliefs are *not* equally valid is as valid as the relativist's belief that they are. For the relativist there is no master story, but relativists forget that even a story of multiple, incompatible stories is a master story. Celebrating unorganized difference is intellectually suicidal, because as soon as we think about the world, we attempt to discern patterns in the complex fabric of the carpet.

At this point in the argument, relativists might do well to avert their eyes or begin talking about the weather. Street-level relativists, though, are more likely to plow on, assuming incoherently that there is at least one absolute truth, the absolute truth that there are no absolute truths.

Contemporary relativism is more often intellectual tribalism. Each tribe speaks its own language, observes its own customs, confesses its own beliefs, performs its own bizarre rituals. According to the tribal relativist, your tastes in movies or clothing, your judgments about right and wrong, your beliefs about the world all depend on how your tribe indoctrinated you. Tribal relativism is a great source of putdowns: "You believe underwear should hide itself discreetly beneath clothes? In what Amish community did you grow up?" If you prefer a Chopin nocturne to Madonna's latest hit, you must be part of a snooty aesthetic subculture. If you think extramarital sex is sinful, you must be a prudish Victorian or over sixty-five or, most likely, frustrated that you can't get any. If you believe that Western civilization is superior to other civilizations, well, isn't that convenient—because you happen to be born and bred in the superior civilization.

Tribes cannot communicate across the tribal boundaries, and when they disagree no one can decide which tribe is right, because anyone who tries to mediate among warring tribes can speak only for his own tribe. No one speaks a universal language. An animal is set before us. An English speaker calls it *dog*, a Frenchman says *chien*, and we can't call on a German to decide, because she's sure to call it a *Hund*. Who's right? They're all right, because "what it is" depends on the speaker's language. Three people try to judge a painting of a rotting corpse: One calls it a masterpiece of social commentary because he is a member of the avant garde; another calls it obscene because she holds to outmoded classical conceptions of beauty; the poor viewer who is innocent of contemporary art retches and runs to the bathroom. Who's to decide? Debate erupts over abortion. The prolife tribe says the fetus is worthy of legal protection, the prochoice tribe insists that the mother has her rights. Bring in the tribe of legislators, but they refuse to legislate morality. Of course, once such relativism enters politics, it becomes obvious that no decision can possibly be neutral. The Supreme Court's ruling to permit abortion does not avoid legislating morality; it legislates prochoice morality.

For some postmodern theorists, tribes are always savages, warriors who have never outgrown beating drums and chests and disemboweling enemies. Disagreements are resolved by combat, and the tribe left standing gets to make the rules for a while, until another tribe takes over headquarters.[2] Many postmoderns are less forthright or more squeamish, arguing that some form of democratic process—that horrid modern invention—will enable tribes to live together peaceably and achieve at least a minimal consensus about truth, beauty, and goodness.

The social realities of postmodernity, particularly the complex of processes known as globalization, have played a role

2. I am thinking particularly of Stanley Fish.

in undermining modern certainties. It's not that moderns never confronted cultural diversity. Moderns met non-Western cultures early on and recognized their cultural and linguistic differences. The discovery and colonization of the Americas, after all, was one of the founding events of modernity, and during the period of colonialism Europeans went so far as to attempt to rule these radically different peoples. Many modern thinkers turned primitivist, extolling the virtues of the natural "savage" as a challenge to the civilized decadence of European life. Yet moderns, whether primitivist or colonialist, operated on the common assumption that *we* are quite other than, and definitely superior to, *them*. Moderns recognized cultural difference without admitting cultural equality.

Postmodern notions of knowledge arise partly from loss of confidence in this modern us-them distinction, a loss of confidence that occurred within specific social and cultural conditions. Moderns encountered the cultural Other, but not nearly so pervasively or constantly or intimately as we do in contemporary, postmodern times. The more *we* encounter *them* in life or virtual life, the more *we* and *they* are mixed together in the same neighborhoods, the less different the two seem. It becomes more and more plausible that *we* might learn a thing or two from *them*.

Cities have always been the main locus of multiculturalism. Urbanization, like globalization, was part of the original modern experience, but urbanization has intensified dramatically in the past few decades. There are more and larger cities than ever before, many of them far from the heart of modernity. Detached from traditional communities, traditional ways of life, traditional marking of time with holidays and festivities, and taken-for-granted assumptions about life, modern and postmodern urban dwellers are homeless minds who can assume very little about common beliefs with even their closest neighbors. Korean Buddhists share a floor with Irish Catholics, ethnically mongrelized Protestants, and Nigerian animists. What will they do if the floor manager invites them all to a Christmas party? Or Japanese cluster together in a Japanese quarter, where they are able to maintain a semblance of the old world's plausibility structure but where they contribute to the cultural and intellectual fragmentation of the city as a whole. Or the alienated urban dweller might seek out creative alternative forms of community where she can share a lifestyle with others of like mind.[3] Whatever the response to this uprooting from familiar patterns of life, the effect is that more and more people live in closer and closer contact with neighbors who don't share their ethnic or cultural heritage. And the trend is not confined to large cities. Even in the small Idaho town where I live, it's not uncommon to hear three or four languages in the supermarket—mainly from Asian and Indian university students and their families.

Travel and communications put us in touch with a far greater variety of cultures and languages than our parents knew, and these same exotic cultures wire their way into our homes through cable television, the Internet, and films. The more we live in cyberspace, the more the multiculturalism of our social world is intensified by the virtual world.[4] Thirty years ago, a black character on a television program was a token, a gesture of political radicalism and a reassuring symbol of the writer's and director's liberal credentials. Now the racial diversity of a cast simply reflects the racial and cultural diversity of our lives. The

3. Lyon, *Postmodernity*, 42, 50–51; Bauman suggests that people retreat to imagined communities in an effort to find an outlet from modern terrors, now that modern comforts of universal reason have become unbelievable (*Intimations of Postmodernity*, xvii–xviii).

4. Lyon, *Postmodernity*, 67–68, for how cyberspace breaks down conventional ways of thinking.

television program *Lost* follows the travails of the survivors of
an airplane crash, a group that includes an Iraqi who is a former
member of the Republic Guard Intelligence forces, a pregnant
Australian, a lapsed Irish Catholic "rock god," a divorced black
American building contractor and his son, a Korean couple that
speaks no English (or pretends not to), not to mention assorted
crooks and tricksters. This is not a nod to politically correct
notions of diversity. It is pure realism. If you were flying from
Sydney to L.A. and fell from the sky onto an island inhabited
only by Others, you'd be surrounded by a similarly diverse cast
of fellow passengers—excluding, perhaps, the tricksters.

Postmodernity is Babel, the confusion of tongues that inevitably follows modernity's attempt to build a universal tower
to heaven. In postmodern Babel, we are always bumping
into strangers who don't share our language, our history, our
culture.

Communications media encourage a skeptical cynicism toward knowledge in general. Especially in urban settings, many
of us are "supersaturated" with media and advertisements,
bombarded by messages from anonymous sellers and senders
whose only interest in us is our credit card limit.[5] The proliferation of anonymous messages tempts the thought that messages exist independently of persons, that the messages are not
communications but mere "texts." The "death of the author"
proclaimed by postmodern theory is partly a recognition that
the author vanishes to nothing in contemporary media. Try
this test: Can you list three advertising taglines? Then, can you
name a single advertising copywriter?

Written texts have always allowed messages at a distance, but
written texts bear the marks of personalized communications.

5. The term *supersaturation* comes from Gitlin, *Media Unlimited*.

Handwriting styles are recognizable, but only forensic scientists can determine what machine was involved in producing a typewritten letter. At least since the telegraph we have been able to have instant communication without being face to face.[6] But the proliferation and expansion of media today increase the intensity and frequency of the experience. Most of the messages we receive, further, are efforts to incite certain feelings as much as they are efforts to communicate information, and this leads to cynicism about the nature of communication. Even the news aims to excite, happily reducing itself to a branch of the entertainment industry.[7] It's all manipulative, all anonymous, all a self-interested effort to sway us in one direction or another.[8] It's like a horror movie: language appears to be nothing more than an exercise of power, all the creepier because we don't know who's trying to control us.

Media, entertainment, and communications can even raise questions about the reality of reality. Computer-generated special effects in films can look very real, and we sometimes have to read the credits to find out whether the movie was filmed on location or in a studio warehouse against a blue screen. This is not the most disorienting experience, however, since we usually know that, however intense it may be, the film is artifice. But media saturation often lays several layers of sentimental commentary over real events, and it's hard to strip down to facts. As I was working on this chapter, the news again obsessed for a few days over the O. J. Simpson murder case. That scandal has always had an air of surreality, but this later episode

6. Thanks to my colleague Roy Atwood for this suggestion, which he takes from James W. Carey.

7. See Neal Gabler, *Life, the Movie: How Entertainment Conquered Reality* (New York: Alfred A. Knopf, 1998), chap. 2.

8. This paragraph summarizes several themes of Gitlin's book. Ken Myers has also emphasized the anonymity of the message-makers in modern media.

floated even further from earth: Reporters frantically covered a media event (Fox's planned O. J. Simpson interview) that hadn't happened yet. News programs showed clips of news commentators discussing the issue, and in case you missed anything, you could get a recap on *Showbiz Tonight*, where media celebrities reviewed the media coverage of the media event that never took place. In an age when the media spend much of their time commenting on other media, in the age of the pseudo-event and the age of spin, how are we to know what "really happened"?

Vapor

The neat boundaries of modern knowledge, and the easy certainties of modern language, seem to be diffusing to nothing. All is liquid, vapor, mist. It wouldn't have surprised Solomon. He would have seen our sense of disorientation and our frustrated lack of control not as the "end of reality" but as our awakening to reality as it is and always has been.

"Vanity of vanities!" Solomon is believed to have said. "All is vanity" (Eccles. 1:2; 12:8). Only he didn't. The Hebrew word *hebel*, often translated as "vanity" or—absurdly—as "meaninglessness" (NIV), literally means "vapor" or "mist." What Solomon said was "Vapor of vapors. All is vapor."[9] Outside of Ecclesiastes, the word is often translated as "breath" (Ps. 62:9; 94:11; 144:4) or "vapor" (Prov. 21:6). According to Choon-Leong Seow, "In Mishnaic Hebrew the word may refer to breath,

9. The mistranslation started early. The Septuagint translates *hebel* with *mataistes*, which is derived from a verb meaning "to deceive" and is used to denote "emptiness" or "nothingness." The Vulgate followed suit with *Vanitas vanitatum, dixit Ecclesiastes; vanitas vanitatum, et omnia vanitas* (Eccles. 1:2), and the English *vanity* drew directly from the Latin.

air, steam, vapor, gas, and the like," and the participle form means "making steam." Other Jewish sources explain *hebel* with the image of "steam from the oven" and take the superlative phrase "vapor of vapors" to mean that "humanity is even less substantial than steam."[10]

When the word is used metaphorically, it emphasizes the ephemerality and elusiveness of human existence.[11] Human life is *hebel* (Ps. 39:4–11; 78:33; Job 7:16) because it is impermanent, because we change and ultimately die. Words (Job 21:34) and beauty (Prov. 31:30) are "mere breath" for the same reason. When Solomon describes "everything" as vapor, he's not saying that everything is meaningless or pointless. He's highlighting the elusiveness of the world, which slips through our fingers and escapes all our efforts to manage it. He is pointing to the brevity of life, and everything in it, which dissolves as quickly as mist in the morning sun. He is saying the same thing as James: "You do not know what your life will be like tomorrow. You are just a vapor that appears for a little while and then vanishes away" (James 4:14). Solomon's wisdom is the wisdom of Jesus (Matt. 6:19–34). The human race learned early about the insubstantiality of existence: *Hebel* is the name of Adam's second son, the first human to suffer death, the first to know the reality of life's vaporousness (Gen. 4:2). In the end, every last one of us is Abel (*hebel*).

All is "chasing the wind" or "striving after wind," Solomon is believed to have said (Eccles. 1:14). Life is a futile pursuit of

---

10. Choon-Leong Seow, *Ecclesiastes: A New Translation with Introduction and Commentary*, Anchor Bible 18C (Garden City, NY: Doubleday, 1997), 101. Ian Provan makes similar comments about the meaning of the word (*Ecclesiastes/Song of Songs*, NIV Application Commentary [Grand Rapids: Zondervan, 2001], 51–53). See also Jeffrey Meyers, *A Table in the Mist*, Through New Eyes Commentary Series (Monroe, LA: Athanasius, 2006). *The Message* translates the word as "smoke" throughout Ecclesiastes.

11. Provan, *Ecclesiastes/Song of Songs*, 51.

something we will never catch. We are children chasing leaves in a gale. Only Solomon didn't say that either. The Hebrew phrase translated as "chasing the wind" is the alliterative *r'ah haruach* and means "shepherding the wind." Solomon's image is not one of futile pursuit but again expresses our lack of control over the world and our own lives. We can no more bring the world under our complete control than we can guide the wind into a paddock for the night. We can no more give permanent form to the world than we can sculpt the evening breeze into solid shapes. Our projects are not sandcastles on the beach. That image, for Solomon, would suggest something far too solid and permanent. Our projects are cloud castles on a windy day.

Life is frustrating, and Solomon acknowledges that. It's frustrating because our temporary, ephemeral lives take place within a particular kind of world. Ecclesiastes highlights the vapor of life, the fact that nothing we accomplish remains. Our projects fade, our labor achieves nothing, and then we die. Yet the observation that provokes Solomon's opening lament is the permanence and repetitiveness of creation. The sun rises and sets day after day, rivers flow into the seas but the seas never change, the wind goes round and round and round, and when it's done it goes round again (Eccles. 1:3–11). It appears paradoxical to say both that life fades quickly away and that the world never changes, but both are true, and Solomon's insight into human life depends on both. The weariness Solomon describes (2:17) comes about not because of change alone or permanence alone, but because of the dynamic interaction of change and permanence. Permanence alone would not be frustrating, because everything we build would remain. Change alone would not be frustrating, because we would have nothing stable that allowed us to recognize change as change. Constant dissolution in a world of permanence is weariness. We strive to shepherd wind and control the vapor, but the world goes indifferently on its way as it has always done. Our frantic efforts count for nothing as the sun still rises and sets, the rivers still flow into the sea, the wind still goes around and around. We are frustrated because the world is impervious to our efforts to improve it.

Postmodern social, technical, and cultural conditions highlight the fragility of human thought and reason, the limits of what we can know, the diversity of human language, custom, and knowledge. So does Solomon. In fact, one of Solomon's most emphatic themes in Ecclesiastes is that the world escapes our intellectual mastery as much as our technical control. Solomon pursues knowledge and wisdom, but he concludes that this pursuit too is no more than vapor and shepherding wind, bringing only pain, grief, and frustration (1:17–18). The wise and knowledgeable have an advantage over the foolish, but Solomon recognizes that the wise and foolish are leveled by the fact of death (2:13–17).

Profit (Heb. *yitron*) is a key word in Ecclesiastes (cf. 1:3; 2:11, 13; 5:8, 15; 7:12; 10:10–11) and refers to something gained, something left over, a surplus. Solomon is referring to the human drive to show a profit, to be in the black, whether financially or otherwise. You write a book, and that is "profit": you leave something behind that will continue after you die, something that was not there before you lived. You left the world with a "surplus." A man who has raised children to productive adulthood has made some gain in life. Human beings strive and plan and worry and work so that they can ensure gain.

In a world of vapor, Solomon asks, what profit is there? None (2:11). The thrust of his argument is that we cannot gain advantage. If all is "vapor," where can we find a fulcrum to gain leverage on the world? The world keeps plodding along as it always has despite all our frantic efforts. The sun rises and sets, smiling pityingly at our self-important activities. The rivers flow into the sea, and the sea remains at the same level, whether we succeed spectacularly or lamentably fail. Of course there may be some temporary gain. A successful businessman can pass an inheritance to his children, and this is profit or gain. But we have no guarantee of profit, and we have no control over whether we will gain even temporary profit. Besides, even if we do profit, someday we'll die and not be around to enjoy or use it.

Modernity is deeply committed to a belief in gain. Wealth can be accumulated, and with the right policies the economy can continue to expand indefinitely. Science can advance until we manipulate genes, take control of our own evolution, and create Superhumanity. Liberal democracy will make us all free, prosperous, and happy. They—the confused peoples of the past—never unlocked the secrets of nature that permit permanent advancement, the secrets that guarantee gain; but *we* have. Postmodern theory dismisses these modern pretensions. Postmodern theory returns to this rhetorical questions posed by Solomon: What profit is there in all our striving? What profit is there in wealth? What profit is there in the pursuit of knowledge and wisdom? Postmodern theory returns to Solomon's answer: Vapor of vapors, all is vapor.

To call postmodern theory's response to this cultural and intellectual situation "relativism," however, obscures more than it reveals. Some postmodernists are willing to accept something like relativism, but most are agnostic rather than atheist. He says this, she says that, and the postmodern does not say "They are both right" but rather "How can we know?" For the postmodern, human knowledge is partial and provisional and has to be held loosely and tentatively. Postmoderns speak in modest "it seems to me's"; postmodernity does not thunder from pulpits. Rather than talk about postmodern relativism, I will talk about *postmodern provisionalism*. The phase, perhaps, doesn't flow so trippingly as "postmodern relativism," but what it loses in euphony it gains in accuracy.

Apart from the sociological circumstances described above, what are the sources of postmodern provisionalism?

Antifoundationalism

Postmodern provisionalism has some affinities with Renaissance skepticism, which dethroned the masterful reason of the medieval scholastics just as postmodernism attempts to knock the crown from Enlightenment rationalism. Bacon questioned the accepted standards of Aristotelian logic, and Richard Burton posited that Adam's original sin was his lust for certainty. Michel de Montaigne was deeply aware of the limits of all human knowledge. He knew everyone sees the world through only one set of eyes and can stand in only one place at a time. And he thought deeply about the unstable connection between language and reality: words change meanings, new words come into existence, and we never have a fixed vocabulary that corresponds in a simple way to the world as it is. Language is never, Montaigne thought, a crystal-clear mirror of nature. Renaissance writers were deeply impressed with cultural differences, and Montaigne expressed a form of tribal relativism when he said that *barbarism* is the word someone applies to "whatever is not his own practice."[12]

While Renaissance humanists were content to know through a glass darkly, modernity aspires to clear, certain, and

12. See Mazzotta, *Cosmopoiesis*, 59.

comprehensive knowledge. Moderns found mere probability intolerable and believed that uncertainty contributed to cultural conflict and disorder. Unless we can be certain about the truth, our disagreements will end in war. Through intellectual mastery, which only *we* are capable of achieving, moderns promise to liberate the world from the ignorant darkness of the past and usher in an age of continuous intellectual progress. There may be a few secrets left, but only a few, and we're closing in on them.

Foundationalism was one of the main modern tools for uncovering the unquestionable truth, which would enable moderns to knit a torn Europe back together.

Descartes, one of the key "foundationalist" moderns, aimed at a *mathesis universalis*, or universal mathematics, that would encompass all science, all knowledge, according to a mathematical model, moving from self-evident axioms and reasoning to certain conclusions according to abstract algebraic calculations.[13] And his ambition was not merely to tame the world in one massive theory. He also aimed at the transformation of European society through the application of this science. The cornerstone of this transformative science lay in his ability to establish truth with certainty, moving beyond the probabilistic arguments of humanists and their heirs and the tired disputes of theologians.

13. As he wrote to Isaac Beeckman in 1619, "What I want to produce is not something like Lull's *Ars Brevis*, but rather a completely new science, which would provide a general solution to all possible equations involving any sort of quantity, whether continuous or discrete, each according to its nature. . . . There is, I think, no imaginable problem which cannot be solved at any rate by such lines as these almost nothing in geometry will remain to be discovered. This is of course a gigantic task, and one hardly suitable for one person; indeed it is an incredibly ambitious project. But through the confusing darkness of this science I have caught a glimpse of some sort of light, and with the aid of this I think I shall be able to dispel even the thickest obscurities." Quoted in Michael Allan Gillespie, "Descartes and the Origin of Modernity" (2002), available at www2.artsci.lsu.edu/voegelin/EVS/Michael%20Gillespie.htm (accessed on July 23, 2007).

But there was a problem. To establish this universal science, Descartes needed to be utterly certain of certain basic truths. Hence the "first rule" of Cartesian method is to cut through prejudice and "to accept nothing as true which I did not clearly recognize to be so." Knowledge, he argued, was "certain and evident cognition," and the science of Descartes would "reject all such merely probable cognition and resolve to believe only what is perfectly known and incapable of being doubted."[14] He was determined to found *our* knowledge on something more solid than *they* ever had. *They* relied on tradition and testimony; following Descartes, *we* would have direct access to indubitable truth.

As the first rule suggests, certainty comes at the far end of doubt. And so, as a thought experiment, Descartes doubted everything that could be doubted—the evidence of his senses, tradition, religious instruction. Stripped of all this apparatus of uncertainty, Descartes believed he could still recognize truth because it would be "presented to my mind so clearly and distinctly that I could have no occasion to doubt it."[15] Once he purified his mind from all the clutter of guesswork and conjecture, Truth would force itself upon him. Initially, he pondered whether mathematics provided foundational truth. It certainly seemed to; who could doubt that 2 + 2 = 4? But then Descartes wondered if perhaps some omnipotent Evil Deceiver had misled him, tempting him to trust mathematics when in fact they are as uncertain as anything else. This became the crux of Descartes' foundationalism: could he find a conclusive refutation of the Evil Deceiver?

Descartes famous *Cogito ergo sum*—"I think therefore I am"—is the result of this process. When everything had been

14. Quoted in ibid.
15. *Discourse on Method*, pt. 2.

doubted that can be doubted, Descartes found that there was still a clear and distinct truth that he could not doubt, namely, the existence of an "I" doing the doubting. No Evil Deceiver could be tricking him here; the "I" was there, no doubt about it. Once Descartes had established the undoubted certainty of his own existence, he still needed to move from that to universal knowledge of the world as a whole. No problem: the whole universal science could be constructed from the argument of the *cogito*. The one thing, Descartes believed, that could undermine confidence in the truths of mathematics was an Evil Deceiver. Since the fundamental principle of the *cogito* proves there is no Evil Deceiver, it follows that we can know with certainty. The argument of the *cogito* shows that the truths of mathematics are just as certain as they appear to be. We are thus delivered from the probable knowledge that contented *them*.

Classic foundationalism like Descartes' distinguishes between "basic beliefs" that are not founded on any prior beliefs from other beliefs that are justified by tracing them back to basic, foundational beliefs. Foundational beliefs have to be self-evident, unquestionable, incapable of correction. The relationship of a particular belief to a basic belief may be quite indirect. There is no obvious connection between my belief "I exist" and my belief "buttercups are yellow." Yet if you contest my confident assertion that buttercups are yellow and try to pin me to the floor with your objection, I would ultimately have to say—assuming I am a Cartesian of some sort—that I believe buttercups are yellow because I believe I exist.

Foundationalists come in a variety of styles and colors. In addition to rationalist foundationalists like Descartes, there have been empiricist foundationalists who operated by a *Dragnet* epistemology—just the facts, ma'am. Whether the foundational beliefs come from reason or observation, logic or experimentation, the *noetic structure* of foundationalism is the same.[16] Some beliefs are underived, self-evident, and basic; all other beliefs are built upon, flow from, or are implied by those beliefs. Modern foundationalism is an intellectual effort to shepherd wind, to overcome Renaissance probabilism and head off any possibility of a postmodern provisionalism, by pouring a secure foundation of unquestionable basic beliefs.

Postmodern theory—and not only postmodern theory[17]—questions the foundationalist enterprise on a number of levels. Classic foundationalism, for starters, excludes religious convictions from the foundation because belief in God, and belief in the triune God in particular, is not self-evident nor universal. For Descartes, neutrality to religious convictions was one of the *virtues* of his method, since he developed his method in an effort to reach intellectual and cultural consensus in a setting of religious conflict. Putting religious beliefs in the foundation was precisely what Descartes was trying to avoid.

But excluding religious beliefs from the foundation is arbitrary. Many of our basic beliefs are not self-evident, known through direct sense experience, or incorrigible in the way that the foundationalist theory requires. You believe, I presume, that I have a mind and, despite occasional and understandable doubts, that your little brother does too. Is that belief in the existence of other minds derived from any other, more basic belief? What is it? I believe I drove by a barn yesterday. I could have been mistaken—perhaps it was a nuclear reactor cleverly

16. The phrase is from Alvin Plantinga, in Plantinga and Nicholas Wolterstorff, *Faith and Rationality: Reason and Belief in God* (Notre Dame, IN: University of Notre Dame Press, 1984). Much of the material in the following paragraphs depends on Plantinga's discussion.

17. Jürgen Habermas is antifoundationalist but also a self-conscious modernist who argues that the contemporary cultural problems can be solved by completing the unfinished project of modernity.

disguised as a barn—so that belief is neither self-evident nor incorrigible. Nor is it based on some prior belief. I trust my senses, but when I say that I drove by a barn yesterday, I am not deducing that from a belief in the trustworthiness of my senses. I believe I drove by a barn in the same simple way that I believe I grew up Lutheran, that my first car was a light green Camaro, or that the Washington Monument is very, very tall and pointed. We all agree, I suspect, that the world did not spring into existence in the last five minutes. But is that self-evident? Is it derived from other beliefs? Can you provide an argument to prove that the world was already here five minutes ago? Our collection of such basic beliefs amounts to a grab bag of logical, empirical, or tautological beliefs. Why can't religious beliefs find a place among those?

Most devastating of all, foundationalism suffers from an original contradiction. How do foundationalists arrive at the criterion for determining what beliefs are basic? Is that criterion itself a basic belief, self-evident, incorrigible, derived from direct sense experience or impeccable logic? Is it self-evident that basic beliefs must be self-evident? If the criterion of basic beliefs is not itself basic, then it must be based on basic beliefs that are foundational to it. But then we are left with a vicious circle or an infinite regress—we have either a foundation (of basic beliefs) that cannot be laid until we first lay a prior foundation (of the criteria of basic beliefs) or an infinite tower of foundations—turtles all the way down.

In this attack on foundationalism, postmodern relativism looms threateningly: if foundationalism is wrong, knowledge seems to be cut adrift from all anchors of certainty, and we seem incapable of knowing anything. But that is not what anti-foundationalism actually shows. It denies that our knowledge is organized in a pyramid and that it is founded on unquestionable certainties, but it does not deny that we can know things. At most, what antifoundationalism leads to is postmodern provisionalism, not postmodern relativism. Antifoundationalism says that our knowledge is partial, limited, provisional. Which it is.

Incredulity toward Metanarratives

Postmodernism has been described as "incredulity toward metanarratives,"[18] and this might also appear to lead in a relativist direction. A *metanarrative* is an overarching account of history in which all local narratives, all facts, and all events fit in total unity. Local narratives are organized by, and take their meaning from, this overarching narrative. If I am a Whig historian who believes that history is about the relentless march of freedom, then Martin Luther will appear as a hero of liberty; the local story of the Reformation has its significance in the context of my Whiggish metanarrative. If, on the other hand, I am a Roman Catholic historian, the Reformation will have a very different place in my overall storyline.

Though all-encompassing theories and stories were not invented by moderns, modernity was a heyday of metanarratives, particularly secular ones. Marx told a story of class conflict moving toward the eschaton of the classless society, and before him there was Hegel, who made up fables about Reason's coming to consciousness. Freud claimed to explain everything—the origins of culture and religion, the deepest drives of individuals, the workings of society—and his metanarrative implied that psychoanalysis was the science that could manage, if not cure,

18. The famous phrase comes from Jean-François Lyotard, *The Postmodern Condition: A Report on Knowledge* (Minneapolis: University of Minnesota Press, 1984).

the ills of humanity. The global triumph of liberal democracy is another metanarrative, and modernity was above all shaped by confidence in the metanarrative of scientific progress. As we unveil the mysteries of the world, reduce the world to manipulable mathematical formulas, and learn to control natural forces, we will be able to usher in a scientific utopia, or at least minimize the risks and manage the challenges of life.

A metanarrative not only aspires to explain and assign a place to all the local stories but offers an agenda for society and politics. Marxists tell a story of social and economic development that puts a Marxist order at the climax of progress, and this story provides a rationale for Marxist political economy. Metanarratives of scientific progress justify enormous expenditures of resources, time, and talent in scientific research. If we didn't believe that science improves our lives, would we put billions into nanotech research? The metanarrative ambition of modernity is an effort to set theoretical boundaries to the diversity and elusiveness of the world, to keep the vapor within manageable limits, and to justify modern efforts to manage the world technically and politically. [19]

Moderns believe they are capable of finally reaching a god-like knowledge because they tell a metanarrative of scientific

19. Modernity, David Bentley Hart helpfully argues, does not constitute a single narrative but a "metanarrative ambition," an effort to "transcend the conditioned finitude and contingency of stories by discovering the meaning, limits, and motives of all stories." Postmodernism recognizes that these metanarratives all "stand upon a shifting surface of dead and living metaphors," but postmodernism is not merely a reaction to the modern but rather the climax of the critical tradition of the Enlightenment, aiming at a "critique without reserve." It attempts also to abstract from narratives and strives toward a status of "meta-metanarrative, the story of no more stories." As Hart points out, the "truth of no truth becomes, inevitably, truth." Hart suggests that a more radical kind of postmodernism would critique the illusion (shared by moderns and postmoderns alike) that criticism can "occupy a place of mere critical suspicion." Criticism is always from a vantage point and is always a type of "surveillance that has determined in advance the limits of every story's credibility" (*The Beauty of the Infinite: The Aesthetics of Christian Truth* [Grand Rapids: Eerdmans, 2004], 5–8).

progress in which "we" somehow emerge from the primordial goo of the past and evolve into something radically different from "them." *They*—darkened generations of the past and present-day primitives—grope their way to knowledge following their tribal traditions, their fives senses, their best guesses and unfounded hunches, while *we*—enlightened moderns— have direct access to the nature of things through our rational scientific methods. Modernity, and especially modern science, has striven to escape the constraints of human knowledge and aspired to rise to a godlike position where enlightened human beings could have a panoramic view of everything. Modern science has done more than strive: it often acts as if it has taken up residence on the peak of Olympus.

Despite postmodern rhetoric, adherence to metanarratives does not seem to be in decline. Militant Muslims definitely have a totalizing account of history, one that legitimizes practices from celebrating Ramadan to detonating suicide bombs, and most scientists still move briskly along as if they were on the road to utopia.[20] It is also a question whether one can ever escape some organizing narrative logic, or whether we should want to.

Postmodern theory, however, is deeply suspicious of all metanarratives (saving, perhaps, its own), and especially of the scientific one. Science has of course proved its power to explain and control reality, but postmoderns are dystopians who unmask the costs of scientific progress, costs in ecological damage, in loss of human dignity, in waste and disorientation.[21] For postmodernists, the discoveries of modern science are enough

20. Christopher Butler emphasizes the enduring power of metanarrative (*Postmodernism: A Very Short Introduction* [Oxford: Oxford University Press, 2003], 14).

21. Butler cites the many misunderstandings of science among postmodern theorists (ibid., 37ff).

to disabuse anyone of its own grand ambitions. Scientists estimate that the universe is one billion billion miles across, and at the speed of light one would have to travel for billions of years to reach the outer limits. How likely are we to explore the edges of the universe? Newtonian science often leaves the impression of a clockwork, geometric, mechanically rhythmic universe, but many of the phenomena of the natural world are unpredictable—the curl of an ocean wave, the movements of the wind, the dips and darts of a fluttering songbird, the distant effects of a butterfly's wings, the way of a man with a maid. And that is not even to mention the uncertainties introduced by quantum mechanics, errors of measurement and calculation, and the infinite complexities opened up when we consider things or features of things not just in isolation but in various combinations. Scientific discoveries have inverted the hubris of science—so at least postmoderns are inclined to argue.

Postmodern skepticism also arises from the intensification of scientific progress: as science becomes more and more specialized, it becomes less and less obvious that it is all one project. The very successes of modern science produce a postmodern ghettoization,[22] an inversion of modernity that produces postmodern tribalism—the tribe of physicists at war with the tribe of biologists, and each tribe plagued by its own subtribes—astrophysicists versus particle physicists, biochemists versus microbiologists.

Alongside these inversions, postmodernism unmasks truths that modern science has tried to hide. The truth, for instance, that scientific experiments require very special conditions and constraints and therefore don't offer the direct and transparent access to nature that they pretend to. Science has acted as if scientific methods quietly seduce Dame Nature to unveil herself

22. Lyon, *Postmodernity*, 17.

to expert gaze, naked and unashamed; postmodernists often see science as something more like gang rape. To take another instance, postmodernists unmask the truth that scientific theories are never as uncontested as the textbooks make them appear. There are always anomalous facts that stubbornly refuse to fit the elegant lines of the dominant paradigm, and there are always cranks who gleefully point out where the undergarments are showing through the straining seams of theory.[23]

At root, postmoderns are suspicious that what passed for universal metanarratives in the modern world were no more than self-interested and oppressive Eurocentric stories. Postmodern skepticism toward metanarratives is fueled by postcolonial contacts, which, to the West's astonishment, have proven that the East and South want to talk back and have something to teach *us*. Postcolonial theory inverts or dissolves the modern hierarchy of us and them. As it turns out, postmoderns note, even the most scientific among *us* have prejudices, passions, fears, envies, prior commitments that interfere with the clarity of our knowledge. As it turns out, *we* have always been tribesmen—just like *them*—telling our own local stories around the ancestral fires.

Historicism

Historicism, first broached in the Renaissance, is another solvent of modern certainties. As I am using the term, *historicism* refers to the rigorous recognition that our language, customs, intellectual and moral standards have historical origins and have undergone historical development. For historicists, the way we do things did not drop from heaven. Historicism

---

23. Postmodern artists make the same point by making deliberately unfinished art works, challenging the notion of "totality" or "completion"; see Butler, *Postmodernism*, 5.

assumes that even the most basic ways we think and express ourselves are products of contingent historical developments that might have been different from what they were.

Your third-grade teacher no doubt taught you that you should write well-formed English sentences, employing proper punctuation. If you don't learn to write with sentences and proper punctuation, she warned, you'll never get anywhere in life, because everything you said and wrote would be unintelligible. Unless you learn to write well-formed sentences and use punctuation properly, you'll end up in prison or holding a sign scrawled with "Please help" at highway exits.

Yet even in our day, when the well-formed sentence is officially promoted as the key to sensible prose writing, there are many intelligible uses of language that do not employ well-formed sentences—lists, lecture notes, genealogies, stories told by children. Listen to a sports announcer for a half-hour, and I defy you to locate a single well-formed sentence. Prior to the modern period, moreover, not only was the sentence not the standard unit of English prose, it was not recognized as a syntactical unit at all. The word *sentence* was used in the Middle Ages but meant something like "sense" or "gist." "Thou speakest sentences," says a character in Ben Jonson's *Poetaster*, and he does not mean that the character "is speaking dramatically but that he is speaking sense and, in particular, uttering weighty, authoritative dicta."[24] Punctuation likewise has a history. Spaces between words were used in antiquity, but at one point it became fashionable to write Greek without spaces, a fashion that some Roman writers unfortunately adopted. Punctuation marks are evident on medieval texts, but prior to the Renaissance there is no "hint in the discussions of punctuation by the grammarians

24. Ian Robinson, *The Establishment of Modern English Prose in the Reformation and the Enlightenment* (Cambridge: Cambridge University Press, 1998), 16.

that punctuation was thought to have anything like the syntactical function of the modern full point or semi-colon."[25] Punctuation in the Middle Ages did not function syntactically but instead marked the cadences and rhythms of oral performance or those of an imagined voice during silent reading.[26]

What did it do to our thought processes when someone (and who exactly?) convinced English speakers that the sentence was the standard of "proper" style and meaning? What gave them the right? Who died and left them in charge? And how has that shaped the development of literature and language, philosophy and scholarship, since? Could there be analytic philosophy—with its careful analysis of propositions and statements—without the prior triumph of the sentence? How is the development of the sentence related to the modern dominance of prose over poetry? If the well-formed English sentence originated at a particular time and was promoted by particular people for particular purposes, what implicit covenants were we entering into when our third-grade teacher scared us into writing good sentences? The historicist who points out that things could be, and have been, done differently can shake our confidence in our way of doing things.

Rhetoric

For millennia, philosophers have assumed that truth and rhetoric are opposed to each other, and in doing so they have set up philosophy and sophistry as the great opponents competing for the mind of the West. For many in the Western philosophical tradition, seeking truth has meant moving beyond misleading

25. Ibid., 22.
26. Ibid., 20–21.

artsy forms of speech to the ascetic purity of transcendent truth. The Renaissance highlighted rhetoric over against the dialectic of the scholastics,[27] but in the modern period, philosophers have often attempted to develop their own technical language, deliberately purged of ornamentation or persuasion, beauty or interest, hoping they could paint an austere verbal picture of the exact truth of things. Language, they hoped, would be a mirror held up to nature.

Postmodernists, in another antifoundationalist move, argue that the distinction of rhetoric and philosophy is illusory and that rhetoric is inescapable in all language use. Language is rhetoric all the way down. Nietzsche's famous claim that truth is a "mobile army of metaphors" has become a banner slogan for postmodern studies of language, put most crassly by the American pragmatist Richard Rorty, who urges philosophers to abandon the pretense of seeking truth and instead recognize that "new ways of speaking could help us get what we want." Postmodernism is the triumph of rhetoric over dialectic, the recognition of the rhetoricity of logic, the awakening to the aesthetic character of truth, the unmasking of dialectic's coy attempts to veil its rhetorical character under the cover of a nonrhetorical rhetoric.[28] Poor Philosophy: it aims to structure itself by "logic, reason, truth, and not by the rhetoric of the language in which they are 'expressed,'" but since the language is always a particular language with preexisting connotations, histories, and limitations, it can never fully express the universality of thought.[29]

27. Rabb, *Last Days of the Renaissance*, 33.
28. This point is emphasized by Hart, *Beauty of the Infinite*. Postmodernism is also an affirmation of the inherent violence of rhetoric, a view that Hart, rightly and with pungent rhetoric, rejects.
29. Jonathan Culler, *On Deconstruction: Theory and Criticism after Structuralism* (Ithaca, NY: Cornell University Press, 1982).

Consider the irreducible metaphors in what appear to be quite literal statements. "How did you spend your weekend?" we ask without a moment's hesitation, and without any recognition that our expression assumes a metaphorical connection between time and money. "He defended his views very effectively," we say in admiration (or disgust) after watching *The McLaughlin Group*, without realizing that we have assumed a metaphorical connection between argument and warfare. "He was really low, but then Helen came by and his spirits rose." Really, now. Our language is infused with metaphor and other tropes, so much so that they seem inherent not only in language but in thought itself. Metaphor is cognitive, not merely literary.[30]

If this is so, can we ever get past the shell of metaphor to the hard, nourishing nut of truth? How can we cut through the fluff 'n' stuff of sophistry and get down to philosophy? How can our language match reality if language is always and only spinning pretty rhetorical webs? Our language is always distracting us with rhetorical flourishes and fictions. Rhetoric diffuses into poetry, metaphors breed metaphors, and rhetorical writing cannot provide the solidity and careful organization we need to have certainty about our knowledge. By emphasizing the rhetorical character of all language, postmoderns invite us to delight in the vapor of language. Postmoderns want to introduce Philosophy to its other, Literature.[31]

30. This is the main thesis of George Lakoff and Mark Johnson, *Metaphors We Live By*, 2nd ed. (Chicago: University of Chicago Press, 2003), from which I drew my examples.

31. This is the formulation of James K. A. Smith, *Jacques Derrida: Live Theory* (New York: Continuum International, 2003), chap. 2.

Deconstruction

One reason to contest the idea that postmodernism is a form of relativism is the fact that some of the thinkers most immediately associated with postmodernism reject the label. Jacques Derrida, father of deconstruction and in the popular mind a prince of postmoderns, sharply denies the charge of relativism: "I take into account differences, but I am no relativist." He characterizes relativism as a "doctrine" or "way of referring to the absolute and denying it; it states that there are only cultures and that there is no pure science or truth. I have never said such a thing. Neither have I ever used the word relativism."[32]

This is something of a surprise, since *deconstruction*, no doubt the most popular term disgorged by postmodern theory, is often seen as almost identical with *relativism*. Deconstruction is—so it is said—the view that texts have no meaning, or that texts are soft wax that can be molded as we like, or that texts have no connection with a reality outside the text, or even that there is no reality outside of texts.[33] Derrida denies it all and claims that he is not a relativist (using the term *relativism* only when, with characteristically playful irony, he is denying he ever uses the term).

Deconstruction is not, in fact, an example of postmodern relativism but a particularly sophisticated form of postmodern provisionalism. In the terms I have set for our discussion, it is a theory about the vaporous character of language, texts, and knowledge. As Derrida employs the term, deconstruction is not a method of interpretation nor an act of destruction. Instead, it is a phenomenon within texts; it's what happens when readers pay close attention to the fissures, gaps, loose ends, and internal contradictions in every text.

32. Quoted in ibid., 11.
33. Derrida's famous "il n'y a pas d'hors texte."

To illustrate: The opposition of speaking and writing, which lies at the heart of much of Derrida's early work, is, in the Western philosophical tradition, explicitly and implicitly a hierarchy. For much of the Western philosophical tradition, speech directly expresses the thoughts of the mind, animated by the breath of the speaker. Speech is closely linked to the presence of the speaker, and so Derrida speaks of the priority of speech over writing as being involved with a "metaphysics of presence." Plato certainly saw speech as a superior form of communication. In his discussion of the origin of writing in the *Phaedrus*, Plato tells about how the inventor Theuth tries to sell his new invention, writing, to King Thamus. Despite Theuth's pitch, the king recognizes that writing will not enhance or improve memory but undermine it. Those who read books will not be wise but pseudo-wise, having the appearance of wisdom without its reality. Writing lacks breath or spirit (*pneuma*) and thus is necessarily dead discourse.

Writing, for Plato, detaches knowledge from immediate presence, which raises problems both practical and theoretical. Practically, a written work wanders off to be read by any and everyone, regardless of his or her ability to read well. Who knows what horrors a bad reader will concoct? Who knows what a Lenin will read in Marx? Theoretically, for the Western tradition, the detachment of writing from presence means that writing is twice removed from *real* reality. Plato imagines a world where thought is uncontaminated by interpretation, writing, supplemental commentary of any kind, where thought is pure thought. That is the real world, the really real world, the world of forms, where Truth-with-a-capital-T pours into the mind like light streaming through empty space. If only it were possible for mind to communicate with mind without the mention of language: that is Plato's dream. Alas, it's not possible. Socrates has seen the Truth—that all apparent reality is only a play of shadows on the wall of a cave—but he can communicate that Truth only by *talking* about it. And talking involves making noises with his body, causing sound waves on the air, using words of the Greek language instead of the pure nonlanguage of the world of forms. As soon as Socrates begins *talking* about truth, he's no longer quite talking about Truth-with-a-capital-T but only about a "sign" of that Truth.

At least speech is preferable to writing. At least speech is breathy, like spirit, like the forms. But writing? A written sign is a sign of a spoken word, which itself is a sign of a thought. Writing is twice removed from real reality, and it no longer breathes. It is a dead letter. Derrida points out that Socrates makes explicit connections between writing and painting, and what Plato's Socrates says elsewhere about tragedy, poetry, and visual art is applicable to writing: All of them, because they are two removes from the real, necessarily distort. Writing is necessarily a lie. So, for Derrida's Plato, writing (and with it all other forms of supplementation) is a form of violence against the original Truth.

Derrida does not accept this hierarchical arrangement of speech and writing. Speech itself, he argues, has all the characteristics traditionally attributed to written texts. Written texts are physical rather than intellectual objects, but so are the sound waves of spoken language. Written texts are transferable to new contexts, where the speaker is not available to correct misunderstandings, but with the invention of the tape recorder, so is spoken language. Written language mediates thought through written signs; but spoken language is as bound up with mediation as written language is, though the signs are aural rather than visual. In short, all the features that make writing "second best" for Plato are already true of spoken language. Instead of saying that writing is a bastardization of spoken language, Derrida suggests that the hierarchy can be reversed: speech can be seen as a form of writing.

Derrida's point is not that writing was historically prior to speech; he knows that's false. Nor is he saying that written language is "more important" than spoken language. The point is to show that the hierarchy of speech to writing built into Western philosophy is a questionable, even an arbitrary, hierarchy. Derrida wants to disturb the structure, shake the theory and see if he can rattle anything loose; he wants to show that the foundation on which much Western philosophy has been built is based on an arbitrary privileging of speech over writing. This deconstructive operation leaves us with an undecidable starting point: is writing a poor-cousin form of speech, or is speech a kind of oral writing? Derrida doesn't push for an answer so much as show that the traditional privileging of speech is arbitrary and unfounded.

Writing may seem an odd place for Derrida to pitch his tent, yet discussions of spoken and written language were quite important for antiquity. More important, Derrida discerns that opinions about writing form a set of assumptions and hierarchies that run through the Western philosophical tradition.[34]

34. James K. A. Smith makes this point with particular clarity: "This forgetting and denigration of language maps onto a general philosophical attitude toward embodiment and the alterity of being-in-relation to others. The connection is a natural one: the world of signs—whether graphemes or phonemes—is a world of sensuous phenomena that activate and depend on the body. There would be no language without air and ears, without marks and tablets. Thus, language is inextricably linked to matter and materiality, to bodies which have ears to hear and eyes to read. Moreover, language as a 'public' phenomenon—shared with others in a community—is an essentially *relational* phenomenon and thus necessarily involves others. Insofar as the philosophical tradition has devalued language it has also devalued the 'media' of language—bodies and matter. Or, conversely, insofar as a long-standing rationalism (and dualism) in the Western philosophical tradition has denigrated bodies and materiality, the negative accounts of language are a symptom of deeper metaphysical commitments" (*Jacques Derrida*, 17).

Speech is breathy sound, which fades as soon as it is spoken. It seems more spiritual than writing, which is permanent and solidly physical. By putting speech above writing, philosophers have been implicitly claiming the superiority of the spiritual to the physical and of the intellect that grasps invisible Truth to the senses that respond to the world. Speech appears personal and direct, while writing uses codes of signs that depend on social convention and consensus. By elevating speech above writing, philosophers implicitly affirm the priority of the individual to the community. Behind the priority of speech and the suspicion of writing Derrida discerns a metaphysical apparatus, which is bound up with a vision of society and politics as well.

The Vaporous Text

Much of Derrida's other work on language fills out this picture of language as diffuse, disseminating, elusive, vaporous.[35] Let's take a Derridan excursion. Suppose you have written a book. It looks limited, fixed, graspable, solid. It has boundaries, the margins on the pages, the boundaries of the paper, a particular number of pages. It doesn't bleed over into other things. Set it beside your coffee cup, and you can tell which is the book and which the cup. It has covers and becomes a permanently fixed object in the world. So long as it escapes fire and water damage, so long as you keep it out of the hands of two-year-olds who like to rip pages, it looks as if it is fixed forever.

Yet in a number of senses, your book is vaporous, and its solid boundaries are not as solid as they appear. You hope, no doubt,

35. If you want the technical terms, I'm talking about Derrida's views on "supplementarity," "intertextuality," and "differance."

that others will read, comment upon, interpret your book. You might initially think that the reader is quite secondary to the text itself. The text means what it means, and is what it is, by itself. It's a book whether or not there are any readers.

But is it? A book that is never read is certainly a discrete object in the world, and if we encountered it in a dusty library basement we'd call it a "book." But an unread book is hardly fulfilling the function of a book. Only when the text is read, interpreted, discussed, commented upon does the book come into its own. So the self-contained text does not seem so self-contained after all. If there is no supplement of reading and interpretation, the book is less than itself. The text, which seemed so solid, so autonomous, is suddenly dependent on something other than itself. It can't be itself without others, and that blurs the boundaries between the text and the world. What makes the book a book? Is it the mere fact of its existence? Or is it the fact that it initiates a series of readings? Apparently, a book is not a pure origin but the beginning of interpretations—and in the introduction to this book we pondered the difficulties of distinguishing between beginnings and nonbeginnings, beginnings and their supplements.

Written texts are wanderers. Once you've written your book, it thinks it's all grown up and moves out of the house. You don't have any control over where it goes, whose hands it falls into, what kinds of readers take it up. As the book seeks its fortune, it could move into a dangerous neighborhood, run with the wrong crowd, be plagued by a huffy wolf or raped by a pedophile. And you're not going to be there to intervene to save it. This is a paradox: Precisely because the written text is fixed and stable, it is portable, capable of being moved from one place to another, handed from one reader to another. Precisely because it is fixed and stable, it is capable of being diffused and vaporous. In an important passage, Derrida says that a written text "rolls . . . this way and that like someone who has lost his way, who doesn't know where he is going, having strayed from the correct path, the right direction, the law of rectitude, the norm; but also like someone who has lost his rights, an outlaw, a pervert, a bad seed, a vagrant, an adventurer, a bum. Wandering in the streets, he doesn't even know who he is, what his identity—if he has one—might be, what his name is, what his father's name is." The son is "lost," "half-dead," and is "persecuted for lack of the dead father's voice." The father-author could help, if only "the son had not, precisely, killed him."[36] Every text is a prodigal son, leaving his father's house, forgetting his family's name, perhaps expending his inheritance in riotous living.

This passage highlights the fact that, for Derrida, all supplementation does violence to the original. Your book falls into the hands of a harried undergraduate who has to read and summarize the book for a class. Supposing she's a conscientious student who doesn't want to be caught plagiarizing, she rewords your book, substituting her words for your words and thereby doing violence to the text you poured so much life and energy into. You chose every word with care, thought through the cadence of every sentence and the rhythm of every paragraph, and then some half-educated nitwit tears it to shreds and thinks she can cover herself by using an occasional quotation mark. If she's *not* a conscientious student, things are even worse, because bad readers will not only change your words into close substitutes but likely mangle and twist your book beyond recognition.

You could escape this violence by making sure that no one reads your book, but then the text is not fulfilling its textness.

36. Jacques Derrida, *Dissemination* (Chicago: University of Chicago Press, 1983), 143, 146.

You need the reader or the text will never be fully a text, but even the best reader kills off your words by putting his own in their place. Supplementation of the text is violent, but for Derrida it is a necessary and unavoidable violence. The violence of supplementation can be avoided only if we can get back to a pure origin, without supplement, but Derrida has declared this to be impossible.[37]

It gets worse. The meaning of your book could change quite significantly over time. In one of his fictions, Jorge Luis Borges gives an extended obituary for one Pierre Menard, a minor symbolist poet, whose greatest literary ambition was to write a few chapters of *Don Quixote*. Menard didn't simply transcribe Miguel de Cervantes's classic picaresque novel; Menard's ambition was to live *his* life in such a way that the story of Don Quixote would naturally arise from *his own* experience. As it turns out, he is able to produce only fragments. Late in the story, Borges quotes two passages, one from Menard and one from Cervantes. They are word-for-word identical, both celebrating history as the "mother of truth," yet the writer of the obituary rhapsodizes on the superiority of Menard. Cervantes offers a "mere rhetorical praise of history," while

> Menard, a contemporary of William James, does not define history as an inquiry into reality but as its origin. Historical truth, for him, is not what has happened; it is what we judge to have happened. . . . The contrast in style is also vivid. The

37. The fact that Derrida continues to think of supplements as inherently violent suggests that he is still haunted by Plato's vision of an unsupplemented origin. It seems to me that only trinitarian theology can accept Derrida's claims about "originary supplementation" without requiring original violence. For some initial thoughts on this topic, see my *Deep Comedy: Trinity, Tragedy, and Hope in Western Literature* (Moscow, ID: Canon, 2006), chap. 4. There is, to be sure, another strain in Derrida's thought that sees supplementation and differance not as violence but as abundance, and this strain brings him much closer to trinitarian Christianity.

archaic style of Menard—quite foreign, after all—suffers from a certain affectation. Not so that of his forerunner, who handles with ease the current Spanish of his time.[38]

Borges is suggesting that even if words are identically repeated in different contexts, their meaning might be quite different. Context determines the meaning of every utterance, and every word of every utterance. Because we exist in time, the context that determines the meaning of every utterance and every word is constantly expanding. Each moment there is *more* context. What I said yesterday will be understood not only in its original context but also in the context of the events of *today*. "I am not a crook," said Richard Nixon, but subsequent events convinced many Americans that he was indeed a crook, and the subsequent events now set the context for the original statement. The ultimate meaning of any utterance is deferred until history is done, until the last word is spoken, until context is closed off once and for all.

But what if that never happens? What if context determines meaning, and context keeps expanding indefinitely, forever and ever without closure, without a last word, without a final judgment, age after age, amen? This is Derrida's view, and he uses explicitly theological language to confess what he disbelieves. He rejects eschatology, any hope that there will be "messianic" finale to human history.[39] Context will expand forever, and therefore meaning, which arises from difference, will be deferred forever. We can never know in fullness what our texts or utterances mean, much less the texts produced by another, because

38. Jorge Luis Borges, "Pierre Menard, Author of the *Quixote*," in *Labyrinths: Selected Stories and Other Writings* (New York: New Directions Publishing, 1964).

39. Here and elsewhere, I believe we see the deeply Jewish character of Derrida's thought. He is a secularized, atheistic Jew who has not only given up waiting for the Messiah but given up waiting for the messianic.

we can't know how the future context, and future texts, might affect the meaning of what we write and say.

This is Derrida's concept of *differance*, which he punningly spells with an *a* rather than an *e* to capture the twin notions of "difference" and "deferral." Meaning arises from difference, but precisely for that reason, meaning is endlessly deferred. For Derrida, *differance* is an issue not merely of textual meaning but of knowledge itself. For much of the Western philosophical tradition, thought and knowledge have been understood in terms of "adequation of the mind to the thing." We have true knowledge, a rightly ordered mind, when our concepts correspond in some way with the realities that are outside our mind. My idea of "tree" must resemble the actually existing tree if I am to know it.[40] But adequation never happens, at least not perfectly. No concept can completely match the thing I conceive unless it becomes the thing I conceive. My concept of a tree is always different from any of the particular trees I might encounter in everyday life, and to collect all the particular trees under the rubric "tree" ignores the differences among all the particular trees I've been acquainted with. No concept makes the tree fully present. In fact, no presence is full and absolute presence. Rather, all presence is marked by absence, all concepts depend on what is not present. All similarity is crossed by difference.

Postmodern theory attributes this dynamic of presence and absence not only to individual words but to texts. Let's return to your book: As a diligent writer, you researched dozens of books and journals, carefully quoting and summarizing, accurately

40. Derrida talks about this notion of adequation in terms of presence, the metaphysics of presence. To say that I have an adequate concept of something in my mind is to say that truth is fully present to my consciousness. I am following the helpful discussion of Bruce Ellis Benson, *Graven Ideologies: Nietzsche, Derrida, and Marion on Modern Idolatry* (Downers Grove, IL: InterVarsity Press, 2002).

footnoting. All the while, not only were you doing violence to other texts, but you were poking gaping holes in your own text, probably without realizing what you were doing. Your text contains so many other texts that it is no longer itself; it threatens to become nothing more than an intersection point for the dozens of other texts you quoted and alluded to. To understand your thesis in detail, a reader will not only have to read the thesis but also follow up your footnotes and bibliography, catch your erudite allusions to Shakespeare and Goethe, read your text in the light of other texts. Your text has become an intertext, a node in a network of texts. The meaning of your text depends not only on the present text but on a host of absent texts.

For postmodern theory, all texts have this intertextual character. At the very least, your ideal reader must be competent in the language you're writing in, since you can't possibly define every word you use throughout your book. Usually though, intertextuality means much more than this. What is the *Aeneid* without its complex of relations with the *Iliad* and the *Odyssey*? Does Dante make sense to a reader who is unaware of the *Aeneid* or of medieval theories about the afterlife? One can read Eliot or Joyce with understanding only with a wide background in literature, philosophy, theology, history, London, and Dublin. And who knows whether some future text will enter into an intertextual relation with yours and become definitive for the meaning of your text? Steven Ambrose's historical writings can hardly be read now except through the lenses of the critics who discovered that he had plagiarized a number of passages. James Frey's *A Million Little Pieces* will never be read again except by the light of Oprahgate.

But if every text is an intertext, what kind of integrity does the text have? Does the word dissipate and diffuse into the network of texts? Is there meaning in this text, or do we have to wait until every text is written before we know what our texts mean?

Solomon among the Postmoderns?

Postmoderns say all human knowledge is, and has always been, partial, provisional, plagued by errors. And Solomon seems to agree. There is so much in this wispy world that we cannot know. Ecclesiastes is peppered with rhetorical questions that highlight the limits of human knowledge: "Who knows that the breath of man ascends upward and the breath of the beast descends downward . . . ?" (3:21).[41] "Who knows what is good for a man during his lifetime, during the few years of life of his vapor?" (6:12). The past is inaccessible: "What has been is remote and exceedingly mysterious. Who can discover it?" (7:24). All human efforts at discovery are doomed to frustration. And so the conclusion is: "I concluded that man cannot discover the work which has been done under the sun. Even though man should seek laboriously, he will not discover; and though the wise man should say, 'I know,' he cannot discover" (8:17). We don't know the future: "For I have taken all this to my heart and explain it that righteous men, wise men, and their deeds are in the hand of God. Man does not know whether it will be love or hatred; anything awaits him" (9:1). And we cannot know the time of our death: "like fish caught in a treacherous net, and birds trapped in a snare, so the sons of men are ensnared at an evil time when it suddenly falls on them" (9:12).

41. James B. Jordan, original translation of Ecclesiastes (lecture, Biblical Horizons Annual Conference, 2005).

Misfortune will come, but we don't know when or where; we don't know what will succeed and what will fail: "Divide your portion to seven, or even to eight, for you do not know what misfortune may occur on the earth" (11:2). The attempt to probe the world, to discover the optimum time for action, to control the future, leads only to paralysis, as action is sicklie'd o'er with the pale cast of thought: "He who watches the wind will not sow and he who looks at the clouds will not reap" (11:4). Some of the most common experiences of life are beyond our grasp: "Just as you do not know the path of the wind and how bones are formed in the womb of the pregnant woman, so you do not know the activity of God, who makes all things. Sow your seed in the morning, and do not be idle in the evening, for you do not know whether morning or evening sowing will succeed, or whether both of them alike will be good" (11:5–6). Horatio's offer to explain what's rotten in Denmark, his "That can I," reflects the vain confidence of a recent university graduate.

Our words are as ephemeral as our actions. "Who knows the interpretation of a word [*deber*]?" Solomon asks (8:1). The Hebrew *deber* can mean either "word" or "thing," and either translation suggests that right interpretation of the world or the word is elusive and difficult. The effect of words is dependent upon the status of the speaker. A poor person's words are not heard, and on the unlikely chance they *are* heard, they are quickly forgotten (9:16). If all is vapor, can there be a final word, a final encyclopedia that will encompass everything and arrange it in neat alphabetically arranged volumes? It would seem not, for as Solomon says, of the making of books there is no end (12:12).

So says Solomon, standing among the postmoderns. And yet he can say that the words of the wise are like well-driven nails, fixed and stable (12:11). And yet he can and does say, "I know," and he says it repeatedly. "I *know*," he writes, that the wise man and the fool both die (2:14), and the living know they will die (9:5), presumably through a process of induction. Solomon knows other things too: "*I know* that there is nothing better for them than to rejoice and to do good in one's lifetime" (3:12). "*I know* that everything God does will remain forever; there is nothing to add to it and there is nothing to take from it, for God has so worked that men should fear Him" (3:14). And he exhorts his readers to know things: "Rejoice, young man, during your childhood, and let your heart be pleasant during the days of young manhood. And follow the impulses of your heart and the desires of your eyes, yet *know* that God will bring you to judgment for all these things" (11:9). Apparently Solomon didn't need to discover foundational truths of undeniable certainty to be able to say, with confidence, "I know." Human knowledge is provisional, partial, limited, fragmented, error ridden, vaporous. And yet Solomon says, "I know."

Blaise Pascal, that most Solomonic of philosophers, recognized two dangers to knowledge: "to exclude reason, to admit nothing but reason." Enlightenment *philosophes* fell into the latter danger, and in reaction some postmoderns have verged into the former (and many more postmoderns are blamed for doing this when they really don't). Pascal, following Solomon before him, wants to avoid both extremes. More fully, Pascal describes the triple demand placed on us who want to know: "One must know when it is right to doubt, to affirm, to submit. Anyone who does otherwise does not understand the force of reason. Some men run counter to these three principles, either affirming that everything can be proved, because they know nothing about proof, or doubting everything, because they do not know when to submit, or always submitting, because they do not know when judgment is called for." To know, one must be "Skeptic, mathematician, Christian," exercising "doubt, affirmation, submission" at the right times and in the right degrees.[42]

How can Solomon, after emphasizing the vaporous character of reality, speak with the confidence he does? The key to understanding Solomon is to recognize that he deliberately limits his observations to what is true "under the sun" or "under heaven" (3:1; cf. 1:3, 9, 14; 2:11, 17–18; etc.). In scripture, the sun is a marker of time (Gen. 1:14), and the phrase "under the sun" is more a temporal designation than a spatial one. It refers to a *now* rather than a *there*. In New Testament terms, life under the sun is life before the messianic moment when the Lord will rend the veil of the heavens and the sun will give way to the light of the Lamb (Rev. 21:23).

Under the sun, during this time, we are surrounded by diffusion, *differance*, death, and decay. Under the sun, the self is elusive, and we all die. Solomon says there is no profit "under the sun," that is, there is no apparent accumulation, no guarantee of surplus or progress. Under the sun, our projects slip from our fingers like mist. Under the sun, we cannot get a panoramic view of the times and seasons, cannot tell a master story that organizes and places every event of history. In this time under the sun, all is vapor—our lives, our books, our words, our projects. All is so much futile shepherding wind.

Unlike most postmoderns, however, Solomon does not believe that the world "under the sun" is the only world there is. One of the things Solomon says he knows is that God will bring all wickedness to judgment (3:16–17). He knows this, but he

42. Blaise Pascal, *Pensées*, translated by A. J. Krailsheimer (New York: Penguin, 1983), 83, 85.

doesn't know it by observation of the world. Observation of the world would lead him to the somber conclusion that the wicked will triumph. If Solomon knows that God will judge the world, that every wrong will be put right, it is because he trusts that God will not let evil triumph forever. Like Abraham, Solomon knows that the God who is the Judge of all the earth will do right.

In knowing that God will judge, Solomon also knows that Derrida is wrong: waiting for the messianic is not fruitless waiting. There is a final word, a word that closes out the time under the sun and begins the time after the time under the sun, a word that sets the final horizon for all words, all thoughts, all selves. And this omega-word is, Christians confess, also the alpha-word, the Word who was from the beginning, the living Word who is with God and who is God, the living Word. The words of the wise who fear him are not vaporous breath but "well-driven nails." For Solomon and for Christian faith, there is a time after the time under the sun, and scripture teaches that there is treasure, a surplus beyond imagining, waiting for us there (Matt. 6:20; 1 Peter 1:3–5). In the time after the time under the sun, there is a judgment, a final word. In the time after the time after the sun, death and decay are swallowed up in incorruptible life.

Not only that: Christian faith is that the Word who is the beginning and the end, the Word who became flesh, has *already* swallowed death in life by his own resurrection from the dead. Christian faith is the faith that this eternal Word, the Word that is the first and the last word, the alpha word that spoke the creation into being and the omega word that pronounces it all very good, this eternal Word who is with God and who is God, has taken flesh and dwelt among us. After all the shards and fragments of revelation through the prophets, God has spoken to us in his Son: he has spoken the Word that is his Son, his final word (Heb. 1:1–2), into the world. Within this world under the sun, there is a Word from the world beyond the world under the sun, and that Word stands forever.

3

The Decentered Self

We are temporal beings. Temporality means change. And temporality and change go all the way down to your toes. Each of your features has a history, and that history continues right now and will continue until you die. The slight bend in your nose—that's from a teenage brawl; the scar on your forearm—that's from a freak chemistry accident in high school. The genes that determine your eye and hair color, height and body shape, are the combined genes of your parents, who inherited them from their parents, and so on and on into the dimmest past. Physically, you are not the same person you were ten years ago, or even ten weeks ago. You lose skin cells every moment, feeding the microscopic mites that teem in your home's carpet and, in return, getting a brand new skin every few weeks. Intellectually and spiritually, you are not the same person you were five years ago, and perhaps, if the first couple of sentences of this chapter have had any effect, not the same person you were a few moments ago. Stopping change is the definition of death—but even that's not quite correct, since you begin to decay—another form of change—as soon as you die.

Where in this whirl of change can you find a constant "self," one that deserves to have the same name throughout the whole process? To what does your name refer? The toddler you? The teenage you? The fully developed college you? The adult you? All of them? But if so, how? Are these different yous united by anything *but* a name?

Perhaps you can find an unchanging someone, the real you, under your skin, way, *way* under the skin, under the bones and organs even, in some cozy, inaccessible spiritual place that time and scientific instruments cannot penetrate. Perhaps the unchanging someone is your atemporal mind or your soul. This is, as we shall see, a popular ancient and modern device to shore up the self against the threat of mutability, but it's hard to sustain. Say your real self is your mind. When you look for that mind, the only thinking thing you can find is thinking *something*, and if it is thinking something it is to that extent determined by particular, and changing, content. You might say your mind can think about the World Series and Dubai's economy and remain the same mind through the whole process, just as the same body can stand akimbo, or breakdance, or do a flip in the air. But locating what is the same in those changes is very difficult. The constant mind behind—before? above? beneath? in, with, and under?—all those particular thoughts is elusive. *What* is the same? Can you pinpoint that sameness and hold it up for scrutiny? Or does it slip away like mercury? Anyone with sense "changes his mind" with some regularity.

Further, your self, even that deep spiritual self way down under—around? alongside?—your organs, is shaped and molded by others. You are embedded in the world, in a very specific time, place, and culture. Human being is being-in-relation, being-there, being-with. You don't live your life in an empty landscape but among things, usually many, many things. And most of your life you are surrounded by persons, from whom you derive much of what makes you *you*. You are capable of reading English and probably, if you're reading this book, know how to speak the language. That is a fundamental feature of who you are, but it's not something that came from within. Your quality of English-speakingness depends on the existence of English, the accident of your birth, your parents, and that third-grade teacher we met in the last chapter, the one who taught you to write well-formed sentences. This fundamental feature of your self doesn't belong to you; at least you didn't invent or choose it. It came from somewhere else, and you had to conform your words to English before English ever began to yield itself to your creative uses.

Many of the characteristics of your self, even the most unique, come from somewhere else. Those elegant or awkward or quirky gestures you use when speaking—they're from your mother. Your tendency to start every sentence with "Um" or "Well"—that's from your father or Ronald Reagan. Your walk is a combination of your brother's and that of your best friend from high school and that of some football star you happened to see prowling down the street one day. You stand the way you do because your feet were trained by a decade of ballet. Where did your love for nineteenth-century French literature come from, or your passion for Indian food, your preference for muted silk ties or low-riding jeans and tank tops? Most likely, these tastes that are so distinctly yours are borrowed from fashionable friends or advertisers. Desires and preferences and tastes are among the things that make you most uniquely you, and yet you can trace nearly all of them to the influence of someone else. Are you anything more than a point of intersection for all the people and things that have influenced you?[1] Where do "I" stop and someone else begin?

Ghost in the Machine

In the beginning was the Renaissance . . .

Nothing was more characteristic of the Renaissance than the celebration of the human person and human potential. To its supporters, the Renaissance emancipated the person from the constraints of the past, from hierarchical conceptions of knowledge, sometimes even from any idea of a permanent human "essence."[2] "What a piece of work is man," Hamlet mused, and in this encomium he reflected the orthodox Renaissance view best articulated by Giovanni Pico della Mirandola's "Oration on the Dignity of Man," who proclaimed that humans' only fixed essence resided in our nearly infinite elasticity: "Who then will not look with awe upon this our chameleon," he asks, "or who, at least, will look with greater admiration on any other being? This creature, man, whom Asclepius the Athenian, by reason of this very mutability, this nature capable of transforming itself, quite rightly said was symbolized in the mysteries by the figure of Proteus." Creating Adam, Pico's God said, "You, being your own free maker and artificer, may fashion yourself into whatever form you choose."[3] Dante's self was multiple, not single: he believed his soul was composed of at least three spirits—vital, animal, and natural—all of which came to life at his first glimpse of Beatrice.[4]

1. See Kenneth Gergen, *The Saturated Self: Dilemmas of Identity in Contemporary Life* (New York: Basic Books, 2000), 74.

2. See William Bouwsma, *The Waning of the Middle Ages* (New Haven, CT: Yale University Press, 2002), 20–23.

3. www.cscs.umich.edu/~crshalizi/Mirandola (accessed July 23, 2007).

4. Dante, *Vita Nuova* 2.

At the same time, Renaissance humanists puzzled over the self, recognizing, logically enough, that if the human being is "infinite in faculties" and "godlike in reason," he must be nearly as incomprehensible as the God in whose image he was created. Hamlet is Renaissance man as much in the inconclusive self-exploration of his anguished soliloquies as in his celebration of human dignity. "Know thyself" was a sophomoric instruction. How could an inconceivable being know himself?

We are not transparent to ourselves, and Hamlet hit upon one key reason for the mistiness of self-knowledge: the inevitability and universality of death. "We fat all creatures else to fat us," he said in a brilliant *memento mori*, "and we fat ourselves for maggots." Death renders life stale, flat, and unprofitable and flattens out the hierarchies of living existence, so that "Imperious Caesar, dead and turned to clay,/ Might stop a hole to keep the wind away." Whatever enduring self we possess is eventually hidden behind the vaporous veil of death. Bodies remain, but they turn from selves to corpses and then, adding insult to injury, dissolve to dust.

Moderns would have none of this. *They*—those benighted earlier generations—may have found human existence opaque and mysterious. We'll crack the mystery and, at long last, fulfill the Oracle's exhortation to self-knowledge. Modern conceptions of the self arose in part in response to advances in modern science, but the responses varied. With the world increasingly explained in mechanistic terms, philosophers asked whether human beings might also be very sophisticated machines. Even some who held fairly traditional conceptions of the soul believed that the soul could be discovered and tested by scientific means. In 1907, Duncan McDougall, a medical doctor in Haverhill, Massachusetts, performed a series of experiments to prove the existence, and determine the weight, of the human soul. He tracked weight changes of his dying subjects for nearly four hours, monitoring respiration and sweat. During the final hours, weight loss was fairly constant, but at the moment patients died, McDougall found, their weight declined suddenly. He explored the hypothesis that the weight loss was due to the loss of residual air in the body and concluded it was not. When he performed similar tests on dogs, he found that they suffered no sudden weight loss at death. What other explanation could there be, McDougall reasoned, than that the weight loss was due to the departure of the soul, a soul unique to human beings? From a dozen or so similar experiments, McDougall estimated that the soul weighed something in the vicinity of a half-ounce to an ounce and a quarter, or, more scientifically, that the human soul weighs 21 grams.[5]

McDougall is unusual for his combination of religious faith in the soul and modern confidence that he could access, measure, frame, map, and wrap it through scientific methods. Others dispensed with the soul altogether. A few decades prior to McDougall's experiments, a French group known as the Society of Mutual Autopsy made a pact to dissect one another after death to demonstrate that intelligence, character, and talent were directly proportionate to brain size.[6] Mechanistic and deterministic images of the self became popular during the nineteenth and twentieth centuries. Modern materialists reduced the human self to matter in motion, concocted of physics and chemistry with a dash of biology, as understandable in principle as a metal ball rolling down an inclined plane. And if the self can be explained by physics and chemistry, then the self can in principle be controlled. We may not have the technology

5. Gergen, *Saturated Self*, 38.
6. See Jennifer Michael Hecht, *The End of the Soul: Scientific Modernity, Atheism, and Anthropology in France* (New York: Columbia University Press, 2005).

now, but we will, and perhaps soon, and then we will be able to re-create ourselves and do it right this time. Behaviorists and some evolutionists today claim that we are nothing more than what our environment or "selfish genes" make us. Even Freud, who stands on the threshold between modernity and postmodernity and did so much to explore the complexities of human behavior and desire, often describes the human psyche with metaphors drawn from hydraulics.

A common modern philosophical move was withdrawal. Descartes—identified by Hegel, Heidegger, and many others as the source of modern philosophy—developed a mechanistic picture of the universe, working from known axioms to deduce conclusions about the nature of all things. But Descartes didn't want to believe that the mind or soul was a machine. So, with Descartes, modern philosophy embarked on the project of distilling an essential, and essentially changeless, thoroughly stable self from the flux of time, death, and decay, and from the lock-step mechanisms of the natural world. The essential self has to be outside history, unshaped by tradition or teaching. Only a very thin wedge could pry apart this true, timeless self from the empirically and lamentably time-bound, fading, eventually wrinkled and flabby self.

For Descartes, doubt provided the wedge. In his second meditation, Descartes applied his method of doubt to answer the questions, "What am I?" and "Do I exist?" As we saw in the last chapter, he was satisfied only with self-evident, clear, and distinct ideas and doubted everything that did not fit this (self-evident?) criterion. He stripped away everything and was able to convince himself that "there is absolutely nothing in the world, no sky, no earth, no minds, no bodies." Only one question remained: "Does it now follow that I too do not exist?" Having doubted all he could doubt, he came upon the indubitable reality of his own thought and the inference of his own existence: *cogito ergo sum.*

The *cogito* not only establishes the fact of his existence but also establishes the sort of thing that exists. While body, sensation, imagination, and other faculties and activities are distinguishable from the "I" that Descartes discovers, his thought is not so distinguishable:

> I find here that thought is an attribute that belongs to me; it alone cannot be separated from me. I am, I exist, that is certain. But how often? Just when I think; for it might possibly be the case if I ceased entirely to think, that I should likewise cease altogether to exist. I do not now admit anything that is not necessarily true: to speak accurately I am no more than a thing which thinks, that is to say a mind or a soul, or an understanding, or a reason, which are terms whose significance was formerly unknown to me. I am, however, a real thing and really exist; but what thing? I have an answer: a thing which thinks.[7]

The stability of the "mind" or "soul" or "self" is a stability of a thinking thing that performs all the particular mental operations of Descartes' mind. The self has an essence, and that essence is thought. Material reality is nothing but "extension" and "motion," those aspects of material reality the pure mind can know without observation or experience. The self, however, is not a machine because it's made from a quite different sort of stuff than the extended space of the material world. It is *mental* substance.

If Descartes was searching for some stability in the vapor, he badly missed his target. As soon as Descartes pronounces the *cogito*, he is speaking about a different self entirely. The

---

7. *Meditation* 2, Great Books of the Western World 31 (Chicago: Encyclopedia Britannica, 1952), 79.

"I" of the *cogito* is no longer the Descartes who was born in France in 1596, who wrote philosophical treatises, who lay in bed till noon through much of his life, who has been described variously as sickly, vindictive, devious, and brilliant. That very particular self could never arrive at the certainty of the *cogito*. Whatever the actual Descartes knew, he had received from his senses, training, tradition. All that was in doubt. The *cogito* brings certainty only because the speaker who pronounces it cuts himself off from the cluttered confusion of his actual life. The Descartes who pronounces the *cogito*, in the very act of pronouncing it, identifies himself with an "abstraction of himself."[8] And this thinking self, this self that *is* thought, is the stable, enduring, fixed self that ensures identity through time. That this stable self does not happen to be Descartes is an unfortunate and unintended consequence of the procedure. That thin wedge of doubt was perhaps too fine an instrument, for it cut Descartes in two.

When philosophers attack the "modern" self as a "ghost in the machine," a "separate ego wrapped in a sack of skin," the "little man in the brain,"[9] they are normally attacking this mythical Cartesian self. Postmoderns unmask this self as a fiction, a featureless nobody, without father or mother or end of days, invented in the pronouncing of the *cogito*. More subtly, postmodernists point to the inherent instability in Descartes' self. To achieve the kind of absolute certainty that he's after, he has to posit a different self from his empirical, public self.

8. Jerrold Seigel, *The Idea of the Self: Thought and Experience in Western Europe since the Seventeenth Century* (Cambridge: Cambridge University Pres, 2005), 59.

9. "Ghost in the machine": the phrase comes from a very nonpostmodern writer, Gilbert Ryle (*The Concept of Mind* [New York: Barnes and Noble, 1949], 15–16). "Separate ego wrapped in a sack of skin": Anderson, *The Future of the Self: Exploring the Post-identity Society* (New York: Jeremy P. Tarcher/Putnam, 1997), 67, quoting Alan Watts. "Little man in the brain": Anderson, *Future of the Self*, 67.

Far from being stable and fixed, then, the self of the *cogito* is inherently schizoid, a madman that might easily suffer multiple personality disorders. One might almost say that Descartes invents the stable ego as an act of will, so that the intellectual essence he discovers is grounded in a more foundational will. Descartes' self is self-generated. Rationalist Descartes is rarely seen as the precursor to willful Nietzsche or action-oriented existentialism, but there appears to be a submerged continuity, a continuity that postmodernists cheerfully unmask.[10]

Despite the simplistic rhetoric of some postmoderns, the "modern" self was far from monolithically Cartesian, and the postmodern self is not only an unmasking but an intensification of themes already found in modern philosophy. In the second edition of his *Essay on Human Understanding*, John Locke included a chapter on identity that laid out a theory of the self that seemed to his critics to dissolve any enduring person into mist. For Joseph Butler, bishop of Durham, the self's identity through time and change was as obvious and intuitive as the identity of two triangles or the equality of "4" with "2 + 2," guaranteed by the indivisibly simple soul. Locke's views, Butler claimed, implied that "personality is not a permanent, but a transient thing: that it lives and dies, begins and ends, continually: that no one can any more remain one and the same person two moments together, than two successive moments can be one and the same moment: that our substance is indeed continually changing." Amid the whirl, Locke claims that "consciousness alone . . . constitutes personality," but this provides no stability either since "consciousness, being successive, cannot be the same in any two moments, nor consequently the personality constituted by it." Butler's critique of Locke's proto-postmodern dissolution of the subject was not

---

10. This is the argument of Gillespie, "Descartes and the Origin of Modernity."

merely philosophical but primarily religious, for if there is no personal identity through time and through death, no one will be concerned with a future life: why care about heaven or hell if someone other than me is going there after I die?[11]

David Hume likewise addresses the issue of personal identity in his *Treatise on Human Nature* (book 1, chapter 4, section 6), arguing that the enduring Cartesian self is a fiction that rests on a fundamental confusion. *Identity* means different things, and Hume is careful to distinguish its meanings. An object might have identity if it "remains invariable and uninterrupted thro' a suppos'd variation of time." At times, however, we use the word *identity* to denote "several different objects existing in succession, and connected together by a close relation." The second, not the first, applies to the self. We are constantly changing, and thus the notion that I am "the same" as I was twenty years ago is simply a fiction constructed by the imagination, because what I really am is a series of closely related but distinct objects. To call this "identity" is to confuse this sequence of closely related selves with something that is truly "self-identical," that is, unchanging over time. What is called the "self" is thus nothing more than a "bundle or collection" of perceptions, not some perceiving thing that can be assumed to lie behind the perceptions.[12]

11. Butler included his criticism of Locke in an appendix to his 1736 *Analogy of Religion* (available at http://anglicanhistory.org/butler/analogy/dissertation1.html, accessed July 23, 2007). On Locke and the debates his views provoked, see Seigel, *Idea of the Self*, chap. 3; Raymond Martin and John Barresi, *The Rise and Fall of the Soul and Self: An Intellectual History of Personal Identity* (New York: Columbia University Press, 2006), chap. 9. Seigel points to the analogies between Locke and later ideas of the "dissolution of the ego" found in romantics, positivists, and poststructuralists, suggesting that what "makes Locke's search for a source of personal stability essentially modern is that it was carried out in the face of these powerful threats to the self's coherence and persistence" (89–90).

12. There is also a process of inversion at work: William James's scientific efforts to analyze the self into its various component elements dissolves the self into itty-bitty pieces.

Rootless Moderns

Not only philosophically but also sociologically, modernity already problematizes the self by uprooting people from the traditional fixity of class and place, custom and community. In many traditional communities an individual's exposure to others was fairly limited. Families would often work together, socialize and worship with neighbors, never traveling more than a few miles from their birthplace. To travel a hundred miles to the capital city was a rare adventure. In modern cities, contacts are greatly multiplied, and modern travel and communication extend these contacts even further. In modern economies we work outside the home, and thus we find our lives divided between at least two sets of relationships—our work colleagues and our family and private friends.

Postmodernity intensifies these developments. Especially in urban areas, Americans today encounter far greater cultural diversity than did Americans of the last century. Nineteenth-century America was not a uniform place, but the physical, cultural, and linguistic differences between Italian and Irish were far smaller than between the Kentuckian and the Korean who might see each other at the mall. Hyphenated Americans tend to take on all sorts of "mainstream American" traits, but the diversity of cultural encounters is more extensive than ever before, and that is a challenge to the unity of the self. The very fact that our neighbors on one side might worship Allah while our neighbors on the other might be passionate Buddhists—if that is not a contradiction in terms—is likely to affect the way we hold our own beliefs, if not our beliefs themselves. We may think Islam a religion of hate, but our generous, hard-working Muslim neighbors make it difficult for us to generalize. And when we realize with a shock that we prefer the company of

our Muslim neighbors to the company of some of the folks at
church, our beliefs in the superiority of Christianity may be
shaken. Even if we reject the alternative views and cultures to
which we are exposed, that refusal becomes a choice rather
than a matter of necessity. Air travel makes the world smaller,
and businesses are increasingly involved in international commerce. All this reinforces the sense that the self is a bundle or
more or less well-grounded choices about whom we listen to
and what we believe. We must become "culturally bilingual"
to survive socially, and this dissolves some of the traditional
sources of identity.[13]

Besides these real-life immigrants, we are confronted daily
by a host of virtual immigrants, peoples and places and ways
of life very different from our own. Through e-mail and the
Internet, we have instant access to a world that was largely
a closed book to our great-grandparents. The home is not
an impenetrable fortress protecting us and our children from
alternative viewpoints and cultures. Through television, home
computers, and other technologies, the world intervenes into
our homes for a large portion of the day. Children of liberal
parents might one day flip on the radio and be converted by
Rush Limbaugh, while conservative parents are threatened by
messages coming through television programs. The walls that
once divided public and private space are being dismantled.
If you doubt that, check out the blog world, where people
bizarrely share their most intimate experiences and thoughts
with the millions of strangers hooked to the Internet.

If the self of postmodern theory has been decentered and
vaporized, this is partly a function of the postmodern celebration of difference. Postmodern society is a multiplicity of

13. Gitlin, *Media Unlimited*, 178.

language games, and as you move in and out of the different games, each operating with a different set of rules, you lose a sense of a unified self. As a result, in postmodern theory, "the grammars of unity, totality, identity, sameness, and consensus find little employment in postmodern thinking. Jean-François Lyotard . . . makes this quite clear when he announces in his postmodern manifesto that 'consensus does violence to the heterogeneity of language games' and that we need to 'tolerate the incommensurable,' 'wage a war on totality,' and 'activate the differences.'"[14] Thus

> heterogeneity, multiplicity, diversity, difference, incommensurability, and dissensus become the chief interpretive categories of the postmodern mind. . . . The consequences of this stance for an understanding of the self or the human subject are considerable. For the most part, questions about the self, and particularly questions about the self as subject, are deemed anathema. As there is no longer a need for the unification of the diverse culture-spheres, so the problem of the self, at least as traditionally formulated, is seen to evaporate. Questions about self-identity, the unity of consciousness, and centralized and goal-directed activity have been displaced in the aftermath of the dissolution of the subject. If one cannot get rid of the vocabulary of self, subject, and mind, the most that can be asserted is that the self is multiplicity, heterogeneity, difference, and ceaseless becoming, bereft of origin and purpose. Such is the manifesto of postmodernity on matters of the human subject as self and mind.[15]

In postmodernity, our sense of identity and belonging is not supported by continual contact with the same set of friends, the same family members, the same coworkers. At the same time,

14. These are all quotations from Lyotard, *Postmodern Condition*.
15. Calvin O. Schrag, *The Self after Postmodernity* (New Haven, CT: Yale University Press, 1997).

this extension of social contacts can make deep and intimate friendships more difficult. We spend so much time keeping up with a hundred online friends that we have little extra time for the people in our neighborhood, and we all know someone whose most intimate community exists only in the hyperreality of cyberspace.[16] The communities we do form are chosen, temporary, sometimes based on common participation in evershifting fashions.

Large-scale structural changes in the economy are having similar effects on the self and the self's identity in time. The "company man" of the 1950s could expect to work his way up through a company over a lifetime and in the process would often form bonds of attachment and even affection that were nearly familial in character. "What do you do?" is a question of identity—equivalent to "What are you?" For most of the twentieth century, that question had a stable answer: I am a farmer, a lawyer, a doctor, a merchant, a homemaker, a minister. Contemporary business practices require a much more flexible workforce, ready to change career tracks at a moment's notice, able to keep up with the latest technological changes. Young people today will likely have a number of relatively different jobs throughout their working life, rather than a single career.

As a result of this fragmentation and fluidity, our relationships become temporary, loose, contractual at best. Traditional relationships are fortified by social constraints, legal demands, and moral expectations. Marriage is a traditional relationship of this sort; it begins in a public ritual, its demands are reinforced by the involvement of family and friends, and it cannot be undone except through a legal process. Postmodernity encourages

16. Much of this is from Gitlin, *Media Unlimited*, 55, 57.

"pure" relationships.[17] A pure relationship has none of these supports: it is purely private, makes no promissory demands; it is free-floating, beginning and ending according to the desire of one or both parties. A businessman on an international business trip might hook up with the woman in the seat beside him for a long weekend in Paris, and then return home never to see her again. A man and woman can initiate an affair in the privacy of a secret e-mail or IM account. Given the low-tech surveillance of eyes and gossip, such relationships would be virtually impossible in a traditional community. Transportation and communication technologies do not cause these rootless relations, but they make them easier.

Self-Fashioning

Self-fashioning is at least as old as the Renaissance, when theatrical conceptions of the self became common. The early modern struggle over the theater was not only a struggle over the morality of leisure activities but a struggle over different conceptions of human experience.[18] Shakespeare regularly dramatized the theatrical character of politics and society. The human world is a stage on which we are all actors, playing a role and making ourselves in the process.

Contemporary technologies of the self have greatly expanded our possibilities for self-making. Your ability to make yourself into the image of perfection is no longer confined to gesture, movement, tone of voice. Those low-tech self-fashionings are so passé. Your body is no longer a given, what you have to work

17. The phrase comes from Anthony Giddens, *The Transformation of Intimacy: Sexuality, Love, and Eroticism in Modern Societies* (Stanford, CA: Stanford University Press, 1992).

18. Bouwsma, *Waning of the Renaissance*, 132–42.

with. You can fashion your body to suit your whim or taste. Michael Jackson can bleach himself and reassemble his face to make himself his sister's twin. Small breasts can be enlarged, large ones reduced, fat sucked out of our thighs, wrinkles Botoxed to eerie smoothness. Bodies become art objects, as ear piercings, nose piercings, tongue studs, nipple rings, umbilical rings, and tattoos become normalized and lose whatever ideological edge they once possessed.[19] Not even your sex is fixed: a man can be redesigned as a woman or vice versa. Women bulk up so that they can match biceps and pecs and six-pack abs with their boyfriends, and men now shop for male perfumes and jewelry. Even if you choose to remain with the body that you were born with, there are few social constraints on how you use that body sexually—though sex with small children, house pets, and inanimate inflatable objects is, for the moment, still (usually) stigmatized.

Your body is a changing but identifiable locus of personal identity, of sameness through time. An eighty-year-old woman's body does not have the same shape or strength or flexibility as her twenty-year-old body, but the continuity between the two is recognizable. But what happens to her sense of self-continuity when, for the right price, she can change not only her clothes but her nose—not to mention her kidneys, heart, liver, and corneas? It is important to see that these challenges not only confront those who choose to employ these technologies and stylizations. You may refuse the surgery that would perfect your face, but sticking with what you've got is now a *choice* rather than a necessity imposed by nature. These new possibilities intensify ancient questions about the self, about your identity, your self-sameness through time. We make ourselves over to

19. On the body as artwork, see Lyon, *Postmodernity*, 81.

fit our (current) ideal of perfection, and if that changes next week, no matter.

Technologies of self-fashioning are not limited to the body. Feeling depressed? Try some Prozac, or any of dozens of other pharmacological cosmetics with which you can beautify your mood as well as your body.[20] Drugs can so effectively and comprehensively change your moods that some users discover a new self they'd never known before.[21]

Fashion provides other opportunities for self-fashioning. Fashion is an "identity industry."[22] Brand labels are tribal markings that lend a sense of belonging, status, respectability. But fashion is a fickle identity marker. If I am going to maintain my belonging, my status, and my respectability as a fashion icon, I can't afford to miss out on next year's (next week's?) fashions. Advertisements channel not just a lust for novelty but a lust for an ever-new *me*. Goods are dangled before us promising fulfillment and bliss; they require no commitment, elicit perfectly disposable emotions, and ask only for a moment of our attention and a few of our dollars.[23] In a consumer society, the good life is defined by the goods I am able to afford. *I* am defined by what I'm able to afford. I'm identified by what I buy, and the continuity of my personal identity is a continuity of lifestyle, forged by frequent visits to the mall and to online catalogs. Nor is this only a matter on the consumption side of the equation. Producers intentionally design goods for their symbolic or iconic value. And so I am made and remade, year in and year out, by Calvin Klein and Tommy Hilfiger.

---

20. Anderson uses the phrase "cosmetic pharmacology" (*Future of the Self*, 121).
21. Ibid.
22. Lyon, *Jesus in Disneyland*, 12.
23. Gitlin, *Media Unlimited*, 41–48. Gitlin cleverly says that what confronts us is less Foucault's Panopticon than a panoply of media-induced sensations.

Cyberselves

There is a residual modernity, perhaps a hypermodernity, in these Promethean powers to make ourselves. Postmodern self-fashioning intensifies the self-fashioning impulses of modernity. Yet the Promethean ambition eventually subverts modernity's aspiration. Armed with postmodern technologies, the Promethean self-making self in some cases turns into something else, as it seems to be dissolved into a no-self. The intensification of modern technologies eventually produces an inversion of modernity's aspirations.

For example: Computer writing fudges the distinction between the mind, Descartes' *res cogitans*, and the external world, the *res extensa*.[24] Older forms of writing, whether with pen and paper or with a typewriter, instantly became physical objects in the process of writing. No sooner do you write something down than your writing becomes an "other," distinct from yourself. To correct a written piece of work, you needed to operate on a physical object—crossing out a word here, erasing a word there, whiting out a line (remember White-Out?). The computer screen is itself a physical other outside the mind, but the words written in a word processor are as nonphysical, or as physical, as the thoughts you are trying to express. The letters are no more than pixels of phosphor, the product of your manipulations of ASCII codes. Electronic impulses in your brain produce (or are somehow linked to) the thoughts you write down, and the product, the words in the word processor, are likewise electronically produced. To change a sentence, you can simply block and cut or move the cursor back over the

24. The following paragraphs are indebted to Mark Poster, *The Mode of Information: Post-structuralism and Social Context* (Chicago: University of Chicago Press, 1990).

word, and the word is gone instantly. It is almost as if you are not dealing with a physical representation of thought but with thought exteriorized, in a form just as immaterial as thought itself. The boundary between writer and writing, subject and object, becomes blurry almost to the point that the two seem identical, and the boundary between self and world seems to dissolve.

Computer communications, in e-mail and chat rooms, also have significant effects on our self-conception. E-mail communication is separated from the bodily cues so crucial to face-to-face communication. Even the inflections of voice and the silences and barely perceptible mood swings evident in phone conversation are absent. Freed from my body, I can reinvent myself at will. In a chat room I can pose as a man or woman, old or young, black or white or Asian or Hispanic or Timorese, and no one will be the wiser, at least in the short run. This disrupts the dynamics of communication is significant ways. My imposing physical presence as a middle-aged white male professor of theology shapes the way people communicate with me. When they can see me, young people are more reticent to express their opinions than they are with their peers, or they tend to express them more tentatively. Certain subjects—the agony of hair loss or female sexuality—are less likely to be brought up when someone is looking at me. If I pose as a disabled Hispanic lesbian in a chat room, those constraints are lost. No one knows better, and I can talk about anything and everything. There is an open-endedness and an unconstrained character to Internet communication that cannot, and ought not, be reproduced in personal conversation.

This does not mean that there are no constraints. Even if I were to pose as a disabled Hispanic lesbian, I do so as myself, as a middle-aged white male professor of theology, with all the

specific features of that real self. But many of the communication cues present in face-to-face conversation are absent. Even if
I am not posing as anyone but myself, I am still making myself
in the act of chatting online in a way that I cannot make myself
in face-to-face conversation. I am in the position of a novelist,
who creates the character of the "narrator" with every sentence.
About the only thing that can be known for certain about the
"me" on the far side of the line is that I am competent, more
or less, in the language of the chat room.[25]

Internet communications permit me to test out a variety of
selves. If I grow tired of my disabled Hispanic lesbian persona,
I can always delete her and shift to another persona with a few
keystrokes—perhaps I'll try something macho like an Argentin-
ian bull rider. In the "public" of the chat room my identity is
various, shifting, a cloak I can put on and off from moment to
moment. But why do it sequentially? I can chat in a half-dozen
rooms at once, adopting a different persona in each.

The differences between web and face-to-face communication
can be exaggerated. We are always "posing" and adopting a persona when we interact with others. As every novelist of manners
since Jane Austen has noticed, we are always wearing masks.
But the masks have become thicker and more concealing with
the arrival of postmodern communications technologies.

Postmoderns are self-conscious of the masks we adopt. The
postmodern self is symbolized by *Late Night with David Letterman*: Letterman is playing a role, that of welcoming, nonjudg-
mental, comic host, and instead of pretending otherwise, he
celebrates the artificiality of it all, bringing Biff and the rest of
the crew on stage and turning the camera toward the audience,
breaking down the barrier between audience and performer.

25. This from ibid.

The show's humor often turns on exposing the showness of the show, with Letterman pointing to and laughing at the mask as he puts it on. So too we play roles, and we know we are playing roles.[26]

In short: Promethean modern selves have intensified until they are inverted. Prometheus is not the hero of postmodern society; Proteus is. And the chameleon is its mascot.

Solomon among the Postmoderns?

You might be feeling the vertigo of an infinite regress: If we're always role-playing, is there anyone playing the role? Is there a self behind the mask? Postmodern theorists sometimes say no, it's masks all the way down, and it always has been. The stable, changeless ghost in the machine was always a ruse. Modern selves, *our* selves, are no more fixed, stable, under control than *theirs*. The self is and has always been vapor.

So: Should we follow the postmoderns and jettison the vocabulary of the self, the subject, or the soul? Does the unified self secede into a loose confederation of selves? Does the self diffuse into nothing, a wisp without origin or purpose, subject to the winds of ceaseless and unending becoming? Is there nothing to which our proper names consistently and accurately refer? Is Peter Leithart just a name for a sequence of successive persons, connected by nothing more than an arbitrary name?

And what of Solomon? If all is vapor, isn't the self vapor too? Solomon certainly thought so. The self is the most vaporous vapor of all. All our abilities and achievements decay, our thoughts and desires are fleeting. Wisdom is vapor because, whatever advantages wisdom may have, it cannot save us from

26. Gergen, *Saturated Self*, 136.

death. Wealth is vapor because, whatever pleasures it might bring, we eventually have to leave it behind, and we can't know whether our heirs will lose it all or preserve and expand it. However much we achieve, there is no guarantee that it will last, and even if it lasts, we won't. "I said to myself," Solomon wrote,

> "Come now, I will test you with pleasure. So enjoy yourself." And behold, it too was vapor. I said of laughter, "It is madness," and of pleasure, "What does it accomplish?" I explored with my mind how to stimulate my body with wine while my mind was guiding me wisely, and how to take hold of folly, until I could see what good there is for the sons of men to do under heaven the few years of their lives. I enlarged my works: I built houses for myself, I planted vineyards for myself; I made gardens and parks for myself and I planted in them all kinds of fruit trees; I made ponds of water for myself from which to irrigate a forest of growing trees. I bought male and female slaves and I had home-born slaves. Also I possessed flocks and herds larger than all who preceded me in Jerusalem. Also, I collected for myself silver and gold and the treasure of kings and provinces. I provided for myself male and female singers and the pleasures of men—many concubines. Then I became great and increased more than all who preceded me in Jerusalem. My wisdom also stood by me. All that my eyes desired I did not refuse them; I did not withhold my heart from any pleasure, for my heart was pleased because of all my labor, and this was my reward for all my labor. (Ecclesiastes 2:1–10)

Solomon displays modernist instincts to control, form, shape, and manage the world. Recapitulating Yahweh's creation of the garden, he makes a pleasure park, with trees, rivers, slaves, and exotic animals (Eccles. 2:1–11; cf. Gen. 2:8–25). But when he reflects on what he has accomplished, he realizes it is "vapor"

(2:11), and his modernist impulse dissolves into a postmodern observation of the instability of things. Life is "painful and grievous": "Thus I considered all my activities which my hands had done and the labor which I had exerted, and behold all was vapor and shepherding wind and there was no profit under the sun" (2:23, 11).

We sometimes feel that we control our lives, and the modern world was built on the assumption that we can control and even improve the world. Modernity is devoted to the pursuit and the expectation of profit in a world of wisps and shadows. For a time, it seems that we can live out this modern dream. We manage a successful business, rise in our chosen profession, plot out five-year and ten-year plans, set a due date for our first child. We often forget that the slightest tremor can throw our world into chaos: a child or a spouse is diagnosed with a serious illness; a hurricane or earthquake destroys the work of decades or centuries; a sudden downturn in the stock market leaves us with a fraction of our savings; there is an imperceptible shift of affection and the wedding is off. We set dates for weddings, not funerals, and that gives us the illusion that the former is more under our control than the latter. When an obstacle presents itself, we think we have suddenly lost control, but that's not true. Solomon wants us to know that we were never in control to begin with. All of it—every last bit of it—was shepherding wind.

Postmodernity is vapor's revenge, the resurgence of the vapor that modernity attempted to ignore or arrest. Postmodern society is a rush and roil of change, and our selves get caught up in the whirl. Nothing stays fixed; every new thing flows on into something else before it can harden into habit. The style industry exists to keep producing new styles, to keep everyone thinking that they have to buy a new wardrobe each year to keep up, to bring shame to everyone uncool enough to wear last season's colors. And every industry threatens to collapse into a branch of the style industry. A celebrity, Daniel Boorstin has said, is someone well known for being well known. But the half-life of fame is extremely short, and to keep yourself in the public eye and keep ahead of the game you have to be willing to make yourself over again and again. Styles live, styles die. Celebrities sit on top of the world for a week but then are forgotten, and they show up, pathetically attempting to regain some lost notoriety by going a few rounds on *Celebrity Boxing*. This too is vapor and shepherding wind. Postmodernity in this sense doesn't bring anything new; it only unmasks the truth modernity tried to hide, that no one was really in control all along.

And that's not the worst of it. The worst of it is death. Jog and lift weights until you are eighty-five; aspire to be the healthiest ninety-year-old in history, but eventually you will be a corpse. Delay the inevitable with skin creams and makeup; keep fit by dieting and exercise; maintain your youthful appearance with plastic surgery and liposuction, but eventually your beauty will fade, and if it doesn't fade while you're alive, it will fade when you die. Build a billion-dollar business, spread your product over the globe, effect a massive change in fashion, but eventually your product and your company will grow old and fade away. But that won't bother you, because long before your company dies you will. Organize and schmooze and network your way to the heights of political power, but soon enough your power will drift away, and if it's not gone before you die it will be gone when you die. Build a tower that reaches to the sky, but someday it will be dust; and if it stands no one will remember your name. If, by some slim chance of fate, your name is remembered, you won't be around to enjoy the acclaim. Write a best-selling book, but when you die the book will have to get along in the world without your help. And you will die. You will end like the stinking bones and skulls at the graveside of Ophelia, quite chop-fallen.

Death is for Solomon the great vaporizer:

> For there is no lasting remembrance of the wise man as with the fool, inasmuch as in the coming days all will be forgotten. And how the wise man and the fool alike die! (2:16)

> For the fate of the sons of men and the fate of beasts is the same. As one dies so dies the other; indeed, they all have the same breath and there is no advantage for man over beast, for all is vapor. (3:19)

> This also is a grievous evil—exactly as a man is born, thus will he die. So what is the advantage to him who toils for the wind? (5:16)

> It is the same for all. There is one fate for the righteous and for the wicked; for the good, for the clean and for the unclean; for the man who offers a sacrifice and for the one who does not sacrifice. As the good man is, so is the sinner; as the swearer is, so is the one who is afraid to swear. This is an evil in all that is done under the sun, that there is one fate for all men. Furthermore, the hearts of the sons of men are full of evil and insanity is in their hearts throughout their lives. Afterward they go to the dead. (9:2–3)

> For the living know they will die; but the dead do not know anything, nor have they any longer a reward, for their memory is forgotten. (9:5)

Death is not a postmodern invention, but death is a—no, *the*—postmodern obsession, the ultimate negation of the pretensions of modernity, the daily reminder—if we had eyes to see—that we are not in control and that progress, gain, is not inevitable. No wonder modern science has been so desperate to overcome death, or, failing that, to remove it from sight, into out-of-the-way clinical settings where we can pretend we have it in hand and where we hope it will never reach us. If postmodernity is vapor's revenge, it is because postmodern theory attempts to pay unblinking attention to death—the dying of language on the air, the death of one thought murdered by its successor, the dissolution of every project, the death of each one of us. We should not be surprised that Derrida confessed he thought about death nearly every day of his life.

And Yet

Some postmodernists come close to the radical conclusion that there is no "identity" in personal identity, no sameness or endurance of a self of any kind. Some have suggested that the self is indeed "vapor" all the way down. That radical conclusion is difficult to sustain, and it entails, to put it mildly, highly unpleasant consequences. It is difficult to sustain because we do experience a continuity of the self. Memory isn't suitable ground for a stable self. We remain selves through time even when memory fails, and besides, memories can be false. But memory is surely an *experience* that only a person with some sort of identity through time could have. I remember tearing my Achilles' tendon several years ago, and I remember this as something that happened to *me*. That memory has to be accounted for, and we can't believe that it is an all but universal delusion. As for the unpleasant consequences, a completely nonidentical self would destroy any conception of moral accountability. If I am not the same man today who yesterday killed my neighbor, it's unjust for me to suffer punishment for that other guy's crime, the guy I was a week ago last Tuesday. This ethical point has obvious political consequences: no civilized society could survive without a notion of accountability that assumes some type of identity of the self in time.

A wholly diffused self is also not true to actual experience of the postmodern world. True, we play various language games and learn to be culturally multilingual. But these worlds are not hermetically sealed, and the overlapping and intertwining of games prevents us from sliding into "a radical heterogeneity of events of discourse and an accompanying pluralization of selves that would attach a different who to every different portion of discourse." There is a "who" that remains across the boundaries between the highly diverse discourses, spheres, and experiences of our postmodern lives, and this provides the "unity, presence, and identity of the self."[27] Alongside (in, with and under?) the various personas I might adopt in a chat room, there is the real me, with all the particularity of the real me.

But how can we escape the force of Solomon's claim that "all is vapor"? How can we overcome the vaporous self? Some have suggested that narrative conceptions of identity offer some help. The unity of the self is not an unchanging ghost or thinking substance but the unified story of the self, or the self that is the character within the unified story. To describe myself at seven and at forty-seven as "Peter J. Leithart" is not, then, a mistake, nor are the various moments unified by a mere name. "Peter J. Leithart" does not name some unchanging core of the narrative; rather, Peter J. Leithart is the "who" that is the agent of the sequence that moves from seven to forty-seven (and, I trust, beyond). The continuous self is concretely manifested in "the telling of the story

27. Schrag, *Self after Postmodernity*, 7–8.

by the who of discourse, emplotting the multiple and changing episodes of her or his communicative endeavors."[28]

I find this narrative conception of the self extremely useful, but I do not find it sufficient, and I doubt Solomon would either. I don't believe that there can be any convincing account of identity through time without appeal to theology. Personal identity cannot be anchored convincingly without transcendence. The modern self wasn't latched to anything transcendent. In many of its manifestations, it was itself transcendent, godlike in its masterful elevation over the world. As postmodern theory recognizes, the modern effort to make the self transcendent—instead of dependent on transcendence—eventually inverts and dissolves the self.

Here not Solomon but the Solomonic theologian Augustine comes to our aid. Few writers have expressed as intense a sense of the diffusion, vaporousness, and elusiveness of the self as Augustine does in *Confessions*. Augustine's ultimate conception of his self, as I read him, is—like the apostle Paul's—radically decentered, since at the core of his being he finds not himself but another, the Other, the Triune God, his Creator.[29] Augustine is often celebrated or derided as the founder of Western interiority, a distant precursor to Descartes. Unlike Descartes, however, Augustine journeys inward not to discover some foundational certainty in himself but as the beginning of a journey outward. His introspection turns into the most radical kind of *extra*spection, as his search for himself becomes a path toward the vision of the light of God. The further he goes in, the further he is led out. Augustine's self, like his memory, is elusive, mutable, pro-

28. Ibid.
29. *Confessions* 7.10.16, translation by Henry Chadwick (Oxford: Oxford University Press, 1991), 123.

tean, and problematic to Augustine. But no matter: Augustine is Augustine not in himself but in his union with God.

John Webster, I think, captures exactly the point that Augustine is aiming for:

> To be human is, on a Christian account, to have one's being outside of oneself, to owe one's being to the being and activity of the triune God. True humanity is thus not possessed identity but rather life in a perpetual movement of receiving and responding to a gift. We are humans as creatures of the heavenly Father in whom we have our being; as those reconciled "in Christ"; and as those led toward perfection in the Spirit. . . . Human being is certainly a-centric, "never centered in itself," and so free from "the circle of appropriation and possession." But this does not spell the end of subjectivity . . . but rather its existence in (by virtue of, through the mercy of, out of the absolute generosity of) the triune God.[30]

Postmodern theory is right to this extent: if we are looking for a stable self, a secure and unchanging foundation of identity, in this world of vapor under the sun, we will not find it. But that does not mean there is no secure ground anywhere. It means we have to search outside this world of vapor. It means that we'll have to fix ourselves somewhere in a world, in a Sun, beyond the world under the sun.

---

30. John Webster, "The Human Person," in *The Cambridge Companion to Postmodern Theology*, edited by Kevin J. Vanhoozer (Cambridge: Cambridge University Press, 2003), 228. Webster is responding to the a/theology of Mark C. Taylor.

4

Power Is with the Oppressor

In the beginning was the Renaissance . . .

That has been the beginning of our storyline since the first chapter, but politically the storyline is somewhat different. The Renaissance marked the beginning of modern politics in a way that, I've argued, it did not mark the beginning of modern conceptions of language or the self. Modern politics is centralized politics, statist politics, and the process of state formation began in the Renaissance.

Throughout the Middle Ages and into the Renaissance, Europe was a crazy-quilt of small principalities, municipalities, dukedoms, earldoms, counties, all of which had their own legal and political structures. During the Renaissance that began to change. Gunpowder changed the face of war, and by changing the face of war changed the face of politics. To compete on the battlefield with gunpowder, states had to raises taxes, centralize power, expand their bureaucracies. Kings began to bring aristocrats who had once been inclined to kill uppity kings into the orbit of the court. Between the mid-fifteenth and the mid-seventeenth centuries, European states gradually

conquered or co-opted the three great rivals to their power—
the church, independent cities, and aristocracies. When wars
of religion rocked Europe following the Reformation, statist
apologists capitalized on the opportunity to argue that only
a powerful central state could control the chaos unleashed by
religious passion. European nations grew larger and larger,
organizing more and more deadly armies. By the end of the
seventeenth century, Europe was being simplified into a collection of centralized nation-states, and by the middle of the
nineteenth century Europe was composed of many of the nations we know today.[1]

At the end of the day, Europe had produced one of the
most distinctive institutions of modernity, the nation-state, a
centralized political unit governing a more or less ethnically
homogenous people. The nation-state was always infused with
a good bit of mythology, especially on the ethnic side of things,
but that mythology was largely accepted both by the populace
and by other nations. Grudgingly or gladly, Frisians, Silesians,
Bavarians, and others agreed to act like "Germans," while
Florentines and Venetians, Tuscans and Lombards began to
regard themselves, and each other, as "Italians."

In the first half of the twentieth century, the two great political
rivals were Soviet-style communism and Western liberal democracy. Though profoundly different in many respects, both
operated according to certain modern assumptions. The Soviet
aspiration to total political control was overt. Economic life
was guided by Five-Year Plans overseen by a labyrinthine bureaucracy; writers, composers, and artists had to conform to
standards set by the communist state or face marginalization
at best and the gulag at worst; political dissent was suppressed.

1. These paragraphs summarize Rabb, *Last Days of the Renaissance*.

By comparison, Europe and America were Edenic paradises of untrammeled freedom, yet Western governments also aspired to control the populace: The economy could be managed, it was thought, by manipulation of credit and the money supply; since the mid-nineteenth century, education had been government controlled; in contrast to the medieval feudal system, Western democracies claimed a monopoly of military power; bureaucratic regulations crept into every nook and cranny of daily life. Both communist and democratic systems, moreover, assumed the modern notion of progress, the opposition of us and them. Both claimed to have discovered the secret of political control that had eluded rulers through the previous millennia of human history, and both claimed that politics could be pursued scientifically.

Management of religion was the key political issue for early modern theorists. Hobbes forged his political theory in response to the civil war that had lately torn England apart. As Hobbes saw things, the main problem was divided loyalty, what he described as "seeing double." So long as the state faced rival institutions competing for the love and loyalty of the people, it could never impose the kind of order needed for peace. During the medieval period, the church and especially its priesthood had been counterweights to civil power and thus caused periodic disorders in political life. Hobbes saw the church as a continuing threat and suggested that the state take over the task of interpreting the Bible. Free interpretation of the Bible had led, during the English Civil War, to all manner of seditious heresy, and the state could prevent a relapse into religious chaos only by exercising careful control of Bible teaching.

Hobbes also discerned a threat in the rising professionalization of science, which he saw as the establishment of another priesthood. So long as there was a realm of knowledge outside the state's control—in scientific societies, for instance—there was a remaining threat to public peace. Knowledge could be "pacified" only if the state managed its production and dissemination. For Hobbes, new scientist was but old priest writ large; it was no accident that scientists also wore white robes and claimed to perform esoteric magic behind closed doors. Even Hobbes's philosophical monism was politically charged: once it is admitted that there are two sorts of substance, matter and spirit, then there is an opening for "seeing double," for double loyalty.[2]

On the opposite end of the spectrum from Hobbes were writers like Milton and Locke who argued that the best way to achieve political order and manage religious passion was to institute a limited toleration of diverse ideas, institutions, and perspectives. The goal was still to subordinate religion to political interests, but the means to achieve uniformity differed.[3] For democratic theorists, religion would be politically acceptable when it behaved itself within the boundaries of private opinion. To borrow the terms of Karl Mannheim, democracies tolerate religions that function as "ideologies," but as soon as they aspire to "utopia" they must be controlled and suppressed. That is, so long as religions offer support for the social and political status quo, so long as they are "effective in the realization and maintenance of the existing order of things," they are acceptable and even celebrated. When "certain social groups embodied these wish-images into their actual conduct, and tried to realize them," they became utopian and had to be suppressed in the interests of

2. I am drawing mainly on Steven Shapin and Simon Schaffer, *Leviathan and the Air-Pump: Hobbes, Boyle, and the Experimental Life* (Princeton, NJ: Princeton University Press, 1985).

3. See the excellent discussion in A. J. Conyers, *The Long Truce: How Toleration Made the World Safe for Power and Profit* (Dallas: Spence, 2001), esp. chap. 6.

democratic order and uniformity.[4] Religions are permitted to practice their private liturgies and maintain their distinctive beliefs and ways of life so long as these liturgies, beliefs, and ways of life do not challenge or disrupt the smooth operations of society and politics.

These clean separations of religion and politics, public and private, were ultimately founded on the modern notion of progress, the division between *us* and *them*. Confused premoderns mixed religion and politics, public and private life; *we* moderns have unique insight into human society and know how to build insurmountable boundaries that will produce a world of peace and justice.

Vapor's Revenge

If modern politics is the politics of central control and the nation-state, postmodern politics means the disruption of central power and the dispersion of the nation-state. The events of 1989 are crucial in the development of postmodern politics. On the one hand, the collapse of the last great command economies spelled an end (for the time being) of the totalitarian political option. The modern dream of a planned economy crumbled with the Berlin Wall. As F. A. Hayek and others had argued for decades, the complexities of economic life make it impossible for a central planning bureaucracy to know, much less to control, economic activity. From 1660 to 1989, modern states attempted to establish a rational political order, but that experiment manifestly failed.[5]

4. Mannheim's theory is summarized by Merold Westphal, *Suspicion and Faith: The Religious Uses of Modern Atheism* (New York: Fordham University Press, 1998), 168–169.

5. Lyon suggests that the project began in 1789, but the effort to rationalize and manage populations, especially religious expressions, begins earlier (*Postmodernity*, 9).

Just as important, 1989 witnessed the last in a series of massive boundary shifts that took place during the middle decades of the twentieth century. I have an old globe in my office that shows a large lilac swath labeled "French West Africa" in the north and "French Equatorial Africa" as it moves south. These areas cover most of West Africa from the Mediterranean to the northern border of Angola. Only a few countries in West Africa—Liberia and Nigeria among them—are outside this vast French territory. During decolonization (1945–60), the maps of Africa and Asia were thoroughly redrawn, as *self-determination* became the watchword for former colonies. Today, that lilac territory has refracted into a rainbow of more than a dozen independent nations. Similarly, 1989 redrew the map of Eastern Europe, not only bringing Poland, the Czech Republic, Bulgaria, and Hungary out from under the Soviet shadow but also pushing to the forefront nationalities that few in the West knew existed—Croats and Azerbaijanis, Kazakhs and Ukrainians, Uzbeks and Uighurs. Boundaries that had been fixed for a half-century and more dissolved, a historical demonstration of the contingency of national boundaries.

New maps made it clear that national boundaries were artificial to begin with and suggested that the nation-state itself might be a fiction created by Western powers. Even postcolonial maps of Africa do not follow ethnic divisions. Tribes with very different customs and histories were corralled together into European-designed nations, and sometimes the national boundaries ran through the middle of traditional tribal territories. Berbers live all across North Africa, in Morocco, Algeria, Tunisia, Libya, all the way to Egypt; the border between Côte d'Ivoire and Mali runs through the Senufo tribe; the Chewa are spread across Zambia, Zimbabwe, and Malawi. It's obvious now that Yugoslavia never really existed as a nation-state but was a questionable creation of postwar Great Powers. Basque separatists violently resist the reality of "Spain"; until recently the IRA was regularly setting off bombs to protest the British annexation of Northern Ireland; Tamils oppose the Sri Lankan government that, they say, never legitimately ruled the island; and there are neosecessionist movements in the United States, preparing to refight the Civil War. By calling attention to the arbitrariness of national boundaries, postmodern political events unmask the fact that the nation-state was always something of a fiction to begin with. What looks neat and tidy on the map was always fuzzier and more arbitrary in reality, an act of sheer power on the part of dominant nationalities. If you think current boundaries between Germany and Poland are rational, you don't know any Poles.

Immigration also chips away at the nation-state, dissolving whatever ethnic unity modern nation-states once knew. The United States has been a melting pot throughout its history, but when guided by modernity's assumptions, it attempted to assimilate immigrants into an American way of life. This was not always successful, but the attempt was made. Today, many immigrants remain unassimilated, and there are sufficient numbers of them to make unmelted ethnic groups a significant political force. Postmodern cities like Los Angeles are sprawling conglomerations without a center, without ethnic or even spatial unity. Religious unity has dissolved, particularly in Europe, where the former Christendom that once defined itself over against the Islamic world now has a large, and growing, Muslim population. I recently read a telling description of an Englishwoman: "She is as English as daffodils or chicken tikka massala."[6] Fifty years ago, that would have been nonsensical.

6. British newspaper quoted in Amartya Sen, "The Uses and Abuses of Multiculturalism," *New Republic*, February 27, 2006. According to an article by Alastair

The nation-state has become permeable.[7] Immigration long has been a feature of modernity, but the intensification of immigration has led to an inversion of the nation-state, the modern political form.

International configurations in business, culture, and religion also challenge the primacy of the nation-state. The nation-state is no longer the only international player on the scene. Nation-states clearly have not gone away, and they continue to have all the paraphernalia of the patriotic nineteenth century. But nation-states no longer have a monopoly of international clout. Of course, they never actually did. All the while nation-states were busy colonizing Africa and Asia, the Catholic Church was quietly going global, growing into a billion-member body and exercising overt or covert political influence. While historians have been distracted by modern economic and political developments, Pentecostalism has grown from modest beginnings to become one of the five largest religious groups in the world.[8]

And now the nation-state has far more competitors on the international scene than it did even fifty years ago. Sport is one locus of contemporary global culture.[9] Michael Jordan

McConnachie, "A History of Immigration in Britain" in *Sovereignty*, "The total of both Indians and Pakistanis in Britain in 1955 was 10,700. The 1991 Census put the number of Indians and Pakistanis at 840,255 and 476,555 respectively, and 162,835 Bangladeshis" www.sovereignty.org.uk/features/articles/immig.html (accessed July 23, 2007).

7. Featherstone, *Undoing Culture*, 82.

8. Philip Jenkins suggests that Pentecostalism was the most successful social movement of the twentieth century (*The Next Christendom: The Coming of Global Christianity* [Oxford: Oxford University Press, 2002], 7–8).

9. Like many other institutions of globalization, modern international sports began near the end of the nineteenth century. The modern Olympics began at Athens in 1896, a few decades after the first intercontinental telegraph cables were laid and a couple of decades before the League of Nations was established. International financial institutions were already in place at the beginning of the twentieth century. The effects of these nascent institutions of globalization were cut short by several decades of world war followed by the cold war. See Anderson, *All Connected Now*, 8.

was instantly recognizable around the world during his heyday with the Bulls, and the ethnic diversity of the NBA and
other American sports is increasing, though still limited. Manu
Ginobili might get his paycheck from the San Antonio Spurs,
but when the Olympics roll around he's back home playing
for Argentina. During the final game between Japan and Cuba
for the world baseball title in the spring of 2006, fans for both
sides did the wave and danced to the Village People's 1978 pop
hit "Y.M.C.A." After Japan won, "We Are the Champions"
played over the speakers. The world plays an American game,
sings along to American songs, and everyone behaves like an
American sports fan. American pop culture, carried through
American sport, is no longer American. Cultural habits, symbols,
songs, memories, axioms now float free of any nation-states,
nurtured by corporations and businesses that spread across the
globe and take their own social and cultural shape.[10]

Increasingly, even policy decisions respond to and are shaped
by nongovernmental agencies (NGOs). Instead of merely seeking national self-interest, the desideratum of the realpolitik
of the modern nation-state, governments are pressured into
cooperation by NGOs, many of which have an international
reach. From her Vermont farmhouse, Jody Williams launched
a movement to rid the world of landmines. She sent e-mails by
the hundreds to government officials and activists, eventually
won the support of super-celebrity Princess Diana, pushed for
an international treaty banning the manufacture and use of
mines, and won the Nobel Peace Prize in the process. This is
classic postmodern politics: a nonelected nonofficial employs
communications technologies, nongovernmental agencies, and
celebrity to shame nation-states into signing a treaty.[11]

10. Featherstone, *Undoing Culture*, 114.
11. Anderson, *All Connected Now*.

The shift of emphasis from national to global politics is evident in the shift of the basis for rights. In modern states, rights attached to citizens, but increasingly rights are seen to attach to persons, regardless of nationality. Mexican farm workers in Texas, Japanese immigrants in British Columbia, and Arabs in London, legal or not, claim rights not because they are citizens but because they are humans. And frequently their claims stick.[12] International courts sometimes treat human rights as more basic policy concerns than issues of national sovereignty.

On the other hand, globalization provokes a tribal reaction, as groups resist the encroachment of Western, i.e. American, culture into their local cultures. The dynamics of globalization and tribalization are evident in language. English is spoken by more people than any other language, though often as a second language, and English words have made their way into many other languages around the world. Japanese techies work at their "Konpyutaa" and click their "mausa."[13] But some countries resist the incursion of American and English words, so that while language becomes more homogenous, there is a simultaneous revival of regional dialects—Gaelic in Welsh and Scottish schools, Frisian on the airwaves of Dutch radio stations, Catalan as the business language in parts of Spain.[14]

Identity politics are another aspect of the postmodern de-monopolization of the nation-state. Instead of identifying with the national group, subgroups promote the political interests of the tribe—whether it is an ethnic, racial, or religious subculture. America's culture war between what James Davison Hunter identifies as "orthodox" and "progressive" is an American

12. Ibid., 82.
13. Ibid., 97.
14. Ibid., 99.

variety of national dissolution. The red state-blue state maps that have been so popular in recent years no doubt oversimplify the complexities of American cultural and political life, but they do point to significant rifts in national unity. Cultural and religious balkanization threatens the United States.

Identity politics have been bemoaned in the United States, but the phenomenon is clearly not confined to that country. In significant measure, identity politics is a reaction to the global spread of American popular culture and American power. Starbucks and McDonald's and Wal-Mart invade a South American city. Many flock to the stores, purchasing not just American goods but a share in the American way of life. Others see it as a threat to traditional ways and organize boycotts and protests against the invading corporations. Modernity's efforts to distinguish between *us* and *them* dissolves as *we* move in next door to *them*.

This, it seems to me, is another postmodern development of large historical significance. Like the realignment of Christian denominations and the relations between the Christian North and South, the demonopolization of the nation-state signifies the end of an era. It's impossible to know what comes next. We could be in for another century of American empire; China could rise to become a far more dominant economic, military, and political player than it has been; Christian nations in Africa are forming regional alliances that resemble the alliances of medieval Christendom; Islamic violence reacts to imperialistic Western, particularly American, power and popular culture, but there are a lot of Muslims and they are not going away anytime soon. What seems clear is that the nation-state, and particularly the European nation-state, is no longer going to be running the show, not by itself. With the spread of easy and cheap travel, rapid rates of long-distance immigration, the intensification of

communications and media technologies, and the rise of international corporations and NGOs, the boundaries of the nation-
state have become porous as never before. There seems little
possibility that the genie can be shoved back into that bottle.

Pervasive Power

The demonopolization of the nation-state is one feature of vaporous postmodern politics. Beyond that, postmodern theorists
sense that they are surrounded on all sides by intrusive authorities. Modern politics promised freedom through progressive
control over nature and society, but postmodernists claim that
modernity brought only slavery. They turn the modern critique
of premodern institutions against modernity itself and proclaim
themselves liberators from the oppressive pseudo-liberation of
modernity. In this respect, postmodernity is an intensification
of the countercultural assault on modernity. The 1960s were,
for radicals, a decade of unmasking, exposing the ugly truth
behind institutions claiming to be free and just. That anti-
authoritarian impulse continues and intensifies, and diffuses to
a wider public, in postmodernity. For some postmoderns, all
authority is oppressive, all conformity to norms dehumanizing,
every "thou shalt not" an act of violence. Anti-authoritarian
radicals fear they are surrounded by people trying to get them
to conform. Power is everywhere, and somewhere someone is
conspiring to prevent me from having fun. It is an exaggeration
to say that postmodernism was born behind the barricades in
the Parisian streets during student riots in 1968, but it's the
kind of exaggeration that gets at the truth.[15]

15. The Marxist and liberationist dimensions of postmodernism are emphasized
by Butler, *Postmodernism*.

The postmodern sense of diffused and pervasive domination is not only a holdover from paranoid student revolts but
also a response to trends in media and communications that I
examined in chapters 2 and 3. Corporations are as interested
in public opinion as political parties are, and they first shape
demand and then track it in order to meet the demand that they
help create. Celebrities travel in clusters of handlers whose job
is not only to protect the celebrity but to manage his image.
With the growth of public relations and advertising, and with
the expansion of the media that carry the messages of public
relations and advertising, we are awash in messages trying to
sway us to buy this and watch that, taste this and drink that.
Propaganda, much of it commercial, surrounds us.

Commercial advertising is grounded, perhaps unreflectingly,
in basically postmodern views of the instability and perme-
ability of the self. If advertisers thought that human beings
were rational actors, self-consistent and centered, they would
attempt to prove the superiority of their product in rational,
perhaps functional terms. Advertisers don't, and this shows that
they believe human beings are clusters of desires, particularly
desires for novelty, for membership in a "cool" group, for
envious looks from neighbors and friends, for a taste of the
American dream. Advertisers also clearly believe that human
beings are susceptible to the influence of images, jingles, and
slogans. Selves are not fixed, and their desires can be manipulated. Human beings can be brainwashed. So not only does
advertising shape desire, but every time an ad goes out that
assumes human beings are decentered, changeable selves, it
reinforces the postmodern view of the self.

Since the 1930s, politics has increasingly been bound up
with media and entertainment, which now determine the way
politicians are evaluated and the kinds of politicians who run

for office. Only candidates with huge stashes of personal wealth or connections with major donors can hope to compete in the media campaign, and only good-looking, photogenic candidates need apply. The days when a grizzled, droopy-faced pol like Richard Nixon could win the presidency seem to be long gone. Political debate is also shaped for the media. We react to presidential debates the way we react to beauty contests: he seems commanding, she looked straight at the audience, he's too fat to be president. Politicians create what Daniel Boorstin calls "pseudo-events" in order to promote their message, and the message is broadcast in sound bites of decreasing size and complexity. Clinton wipes a tear for the camera to italicize his sincerity; "W." dons a flak jacket he never wore in combat to enhance his image as a tough-as-Texas war president.

Pseudo-events are not always as simple as a camera shot. Jean Baudrillard famously claimed that the first Gulf War was such a pseudo-event, a virtual war that was more virtual than war, more media than event. If he meant that there were no troops in Kuwait, no bombs were dropped, no buildings in Baghdad destroyed, he was wrong. That all took place. But the war's meaning and impact in the United States were filtered by media coverage—special reports on cool military technologies like smart bombs, press conferences with the entertaining, comfortingly avuncular General Schwartzkopf, visuals of targeted infrastructure or Iraqi missiles launching aimlessly from Baghdad into the night sky. Besides, the war, like the 1983 U.S. invasion of Grenada, was designed not only to secure Kuwait and force Saddam Hussein into retreat but to project an image of America to the world, particularly the Muslim world.[16] War

16. Anderson, *Reality Isn't What It Used to Be*, 125–26, on Grenada as a media event.

broadcast on TV becomes hard to distinguish from image making and entertainment.

Yet the postmodern political situation is complicated by the fact that *we* know *they* know they are being watched. If media and advertising create jaded and cynical viewers, they also create a jaded and cynical citizenry. Politicians seek to promote themselves through media organs, but knowing viewers are suspicious of being manipulated. Sound bites of ever-shorter duration pass for political news, but everyone now knows that sounds bites are concocted for public consumption.[17] We viewers know politicians, editors, reporters are shaping the news to their purposes. We know that presidents meet with media consultants along with other advisers to determine what message will sell and that they go to makeup just like actors before they appear in presidential debates. We know that they are striving to shape public opinion, to exercise power through the diffused and omnipresent media. We become ironic viewers, entering into implicit alliances with ironic politicians who rarely say openly what they intend to do or what they are about.

Political theater and image mongering are not confined to politicians. Protest events are concocted for the cameras. This is part of the reason that radicals are so rapidly and smoothly co-opted by postmodern society, particularly in the United States. A radical raging at the system gets on camera, and his passion makes for good television. He's an instant star, and the big news agencies—whose interest is as much in profits as in distributing information—want to keep him on camera as much as possible. They follow his every move, they deploy a team of reporters and tech people for a documentary, and before you know it the radical has become part of the

17. Gitlin, *Media Unlimited*, 121.

mainstream. Soon enough he's running for president. Can you say Al Sharpton?

Liberating Knowledge

Postmodern political theory expresses this unease with all-pervading media manipulation. Postmoderns consider power, and often violence, to be a pervasive reality in social life. For postmoderns, power has diffused like vapor. It's part of the air we, all of us, breathe. Contrary to modern mythologies, modern democracies did not achieve real freedom. Modern democracies only constructed clever new ways of controlling people. Postmoderns unmask modern liberty as a form of domination. Where moderns claimed to provide freedom over against the institutionalized slavery of the past, postmoderns recognize that *our* politics were never so different from *theirs*.

Against the modern obsession with questions of sovereignty, legitimacy, and the rights of centralized power, for instance, Michel Foucault, one of the major voices of postmodern theory, concentrates attention on local and specific mechanics, strategies, tactics of power—an economy of power that flows in and around human life and shapes all human relationships. Although the remaining monarchs of European nations are powerless figureheads, political theory still operates, Foucault argues, as if power radiated out from a courtly center: "We need to cut off the King's head: in political theory that has still to be done."[18] Operating on similar assumptions, theorists and artists see their work as inherently political. Liberal democra-

18. Michel Foucault, *Power/Knowledge: Selective Interviews and Other Writings, 1972–1977*, edited by Colin Gordon (New York: Pantheon, 1980), 121.

cies separated the public realm of coercion and policy from a private realm of free expression; postmoderns see through the ruse of the private realm. For postmoderns, the private realm is also suffused with politics.[19] Postmoderns unmask the truth that modernity's separation of public and private was never as clean as modernity claimed.

Foucault saw his project not only as an assault on modern obsessions with questions of centralized power and sovereignty but also (and, interestingly, quite "modernly") as an effort to liberate "subjugated knowledges." Some areas of study were marginalized and suppressed because modern theorists pursued grand, unitary theories, casting aside all the losing theories and setting inconvenient facts on shelves to gather dust. The dominance of scientific discourse subjected knowledge that didn't qualify as "scientific." Modern theory has, as a result, excluded "a whole set of knowledges that have been disqualified as inadequate to their task or insufficiently elaborated: naïve knowledges, located low down on the hierarchy, beneath the required level of cognition or scientificity." What Foucault calls "low-ranking knowledges" include knowledge from the side of the subject of theory as opposed to theorist—the knowledge of the psychiatric patient as opposed to the psychoanalyst, the knowledge of the sick person, attending nurse, and doctor as opposed to the official knowledge of the hospital and medical textbooks, the knowledge of the criminal as opposed to that of the police and the courts.[20]

Unitary, totalizing theories are written by the victors. Psychiatric history is told by those whose theories became dominant, and earlier debates are often described as if they were a smooth preparation for the triumphant theory. When disqualified or

---

19. See Butler, *Postmodernism*, 78–84, on conceptualism in art.
20. Foucault, *Power/Knowledge*, 81–82.

subjugated knowledges are taken into account, however, it becomes evident that there is no elegantly teleological story to tell. The development of the institutions and fields of knowledge that moderns take for granted takes place through struggles and battles. Foucault's genealogical method seeks "the union of erudite knowledge and local memories which allows us to establish a historical knowledge of struggles and to make use of this knowledge tactically today."[21] Foucault saw his own academic work as an act of emancipation for ignored and forgotten discourses and fields of knowledge, and he believed that uncovering the struggles of the past can liberate us even now by calling into question the dominant discourses of the present.

From Spectacle to Surveillance

Foucault's rhetoric sometimes gets away from him, but his description of power relations diffused throughout society gets at important and genuinely neglected features of human life and modern history. In a brilliant chapter of *Discipline and Punish*, Foucault recounts how disciplines exercised through spatial and temporal organization produced "docile bodies" in various institutions. Discipline was exercised by enclosing subjects in an environment—a factory, school, hospital, military barracks—where individuals were partitioned from each other to prevent unruly groups from gathering together. Not only persons but architectural spaces were partitioned among different functions. Enclosure and partitioning made it possible for the authorities to supervise (to "look-over") those subjected to their discipline. Activities were subjected to disciplines through

21. Ibid., 83.

the organization of time—rigorous schedules, temporally regi-
mented activities like marching or exercises, the breakdown
of actions into a sequence of subactions that must be repeated
again and again until the body acts automatically (the basketball
shot broken down into different bodily movements—cock arm,
elbow in, flick wrist, follow-through—and a changing relation
to the ball).[22] Infractions were punished: "The workshop, the
school, the army were subject to a whole micro-penality of time
(latenesses, absences, interruptions of tasks), of activity (inat-
tention, negligence, lack of zeal), of behaviour (impoliteness,
disobedience), of speech (idle chatter, insolence), of the body
('incorrect' attitudes, irregular gestures, lack of cleanliness), of
sexuality (impurity, indecency)."[23] As a result of these spatial,
temporal, and behavioral disciplines, the members of the group
conformed to a particular pattern of conduct. Schools, hospitals, the military, and prisons produced new persons, a newly
disciplined style of being human. Discipline forged a collection
of individuals into a human architecture, a living machine in
which each individual became a cog. Screened from public view,
those who exercised discipline were also interchangeable.

This last illustrates Foucault's notion of "Panopticism," a
concept he derived from Jeremy Bentham's visionary proposal
for prison reform. In place of traditional prison arrangements,
Bentham imagined a prison whose cells surrounded and opened
into a central court. At the center of the court is the Panopticon,
a tower that serves as the all-seeing center of surveillance for
prison authorities, who can watch each prisoner whenever they
please. Of course, those in the surveillance tower can't keep
track of all the prisoners all the time; it would be prohibitively

22. Foucault, *Discipline and Punish: The Birth of the Prison*, translated by Alan
Sheridan (New York: Vintage, 1979), 141–56.
    23. Ibid., 178.

expensive to hire at least two or three guards per prisoner to keep each under constant observation. But the discipline imposed by the Panopticon doesn't depend on keeping the prisoners under 24/7 surveillance. The *possibility* that they might be watched is enough to keep them on their best behavior.

Bentham's model is referred to in nearly every treatise and tract on prison reform produced in the eighteenth and nineteenth centuries and that same model was applied to hospitals, factories, and schools. Disciplinary power was exercised in local ways through the strategies, mechanisms, and techniques provided by the spatial arrangements of the Panopticon. The Panopticon provided not only a model for small-scale institutions but an aspiration for a nation as a whole, the aspiration to keep the whole population under surveillance through census taking, tax codes, receipts, and other bureaucratic mechanisms. The Panopticon serves as a "figure of political technology" that can be transferred from one institution to another.[24]

This elevation of the Panoptic model is part of the major shift that Foucault traces in his history of punishments and prisons. He begins his book *Discipline and Punish* with an infamously horrific description of the public execution of Damiens the regicide in 1757, and from there his book traces the development of prison reform. As told by modern historians, the story of prison reform is one of increasing humanitarianism, as reformers disgusted by the cruelty of punishment and incarceration heroically constructed a system that would emphasize rehabilitation and humane treatment of prisoners. Foucault sees something far more sinister going on. Prison reform is not a move from cruelty to humane forms of punishment, but merely a shift in the mechanisms and strategies of power, a

24. Ibid., 205.

shift that he describes in terms of a change from punishment to discipline and from spectacle to surveillance.

Prior to the eighteenth century, power was exercised by spectacle—through monumental architecture, through grotesque public executions, through displays of royal wealth and luxury. Subjects were overawed when they turned their eyes to the glories of the sovereign. Cruel and extended public torture was designed not merely to punish the convicted criminal but to send a message of shock and awe to everyone in the crowd. During the eighteenth and nineteenth centuries, cruel punishments were eliminated, but the exercise of power continued through other means. Surveillance replaced spectacle as the mechanism of power. Since the eighteenth century, the direction of sight has been reversed. Our rulers don't try to overawe us with displays of glory. They seek to instill self-discipline through the threat that at any moment they might be watching us.

Marx and Postmodernism

The intellectual impetus behind postmodern theories of power and politics has been generically Marxist. Marx had a large presence in French thought during the early twentieth century, and even after the devastating revelations of Aleksandr Solzhenitsyn, French intellectuals often continued to work in a Marxist framework. Questioned about his debts to Marx, Foucault said that he used Marx more than quoted him and suggested that "it is impossible at the present time to write history without using a whole range of concepts directly or indirectly linked to Marx's thought. . . . One might even wonder what difference there could ultimately be between being a historian and being a Marxist."[25]

25. Foucault, *Power/Knowledge*, 53.

Though muted in Marx's own work and never precisely defined there, the concept of "ideology" has been prominent in later Marxist writers and among the postmodern users of Marx. In talking about ideology, Marx and his followers are concerned not so much with the truth of the ideas expressed as with the function of those ideas in society.[26] For Marx, social structures are based on economic relations, and "legal and political superstructure arise[s]" from these economically based social structures, to which are added "definite forms of social consciousness." Thus "the mode of production of material life determines the general character of the social, political and spiritual processes of life. It is not the consciousness of men that determines their being, but, on the contrary, their social being determines their consciousness." Changes in the economic substructure cause changes in the superstructure as well, in the "legal, political, religious, aesthetic or philosophical—in short ideological, forms in which men become conscious of this conflict and fight it out."[27] Ideas are founded on economic relations. They are not arrived at by a dispassionate and neutral analysis of the world but arise from class interests.

Views in religion, economic theories, historical myths, laws, utopian political programs become ideological when people forget that their ideas have originated in particular social conditions and fail to see how they function in society.[28] Dominant classes are not identified simply by ownership of the means of production but also by their control over various forms of cultural and social capital. A class might possess dominance over

26. I take this helpful distinction from Westphal, *Suspicion and Faith*.

27. Karl Marx, *Selected Writings in Sociology and Social Philosophy*, translated and edited by T. B. Bottomore (New York: McGraw-Hill, 1956), 51. The selection is taken from *The German Ideology*.

28. Leszek Kolakowski, *Main Currents of Marxism*, 3 vols. in 1 (New York: W. W. Norton, 2005), 127.

the production and distribution of symbols as well as over the production and distributions of physical goods, and the classes that dominate symbolic production and distribution are as self-protective as is Marx's economic bourgeoisie. What ideologues forget is the fact that dominant ideas express the interests of a dominant class and function to preserve those interests.

One postmodern theorist, Louis Althusser, combined structuralism with a Marxist emphasis on ideology, arguing that discourse "interpellates" the individual, placing him in a particular role that serves the interests of the ruling class. Suppose males are dominant in some society. To protect their hegemony, men knowingly and unknowingly promote an ideology that underwrites their status. Their very discourse "interpellates" women in a subordinate position, as with the grammatical convention of employing masculine indefinite pronouns. Children's picture books show women in domestic roles, once again interpellating them in their social role. These are not, postmoderns argue, innocent grammatical or pictorial conventions. Every grammatical decision, every discourse, is an act of power promoted by the male-dominated world of grammarians. Discourses are acts of violence against the oppressed that pressure individuals to conform to prescribed social roles.

If postmodern political theory is Marxist, it is de-eschatologized Marxism. Marx prophesied that someday the capitalist system would collapse into a dictatorship of the proletariat and eventually yield to a classless society, an Edenic land of Cockaigne. Postmoderns embrace Marx's cynicism about power, but they will have none of his eschatology. Postmodern Marxist is undermined by a noble Nietzschean despair, which ultimately belies postmodernity's quite modern promise of liberation. Foucault mocks the pretenses of modern freedom but claims that somehow his own genealogies will be emancipatory. Then again, maybe not; because he also assumes that every regime, regardless of the form it takes, is nothing but a structure of domination precisely because it's a regime. Power is by definition with the oppressor, postmodern theorists say, and that's just where it always stays.

Power, Self, Language

Postmodern conceptions of the self are thus bound up with notions of power. The self is a "subject," not only in the philosophical sense of "subjectivity" but in the political sense of "subjection to." For many postmodern thinkers, the self is the product of the pressures of power. The self is made, becomes a subject, by subjection to the dominant class or ideology. Foucault claims that "the individual, with his identity and characteristics, is the product of a relation of power exercised over bodies, multiplicities, movements, desires, forces."[29]

In some respects this is a sociological truism, but as Christopher Butler explains, postmodern theorists aim at something more radical.

> Of course, the fact that institutions and their discourses demand that you be a particular sort of person, to "fit in," was hardly unknown. Anyone who has been in a school or a sports team or a military organization or given birth to a baby in a hospital, let alone read some of the "Organization Man" sociology of the 1950s, is to some degree aware of this point. But the postmodernist argument was an exceptionally subtle one. We don't just *play roles* in such cases, but our very identity, the notion we have of ourselves, is at issue when we are affected by discourses of power. These, of course, run from those which are directly

29. Foucault, *Power/Knowledge*, 74.

concerned with matters of identity (in religion, and in therapy from Freudianism to psycho-babble), to those which are far less obviously so, as in the case of a woman responding to the female lead in a male-dominated Hollywood film, or to paintings of the nude in the male-dominated museum, or the teenager in front of the TV set. All discourses put you in your place.[30]

For postmodern theorists like Foucault, discourses do not shape a preexisting subject by adding characteristics and features and personality traits. Foucault distinguishes his theory from that of phenomenologists who argue that the subject "evolves through the course of history." Instead, "one has to dispense with the constituent subject, to get rid of the subject itself," which means to treat the "constitution of the subject within a historical framework."[31] There is no "basic subject" beneath the subject created by subjection. There is *only* the subject who has been created by subjection.

But the subjection exercised in postmodern society is multiple. Discourses are diverse, and the variety of shaping discourses is part of the reason that postmodernists view the self as "decentered." If discourses constitute us as "subjects" and we are subjected to dozens of competing discourses, then it follows that we are going to be multiple rather than unified, schizophrenic rather than integrated personalities. We are subjected to discourses that promote the interests of political leaders, advertisers, and film and TV producers, not to mention the multiple discourses that we encounter in our culturally diverse daily lives.

Postmodernism's obsession with power is evident, further, in one of the most widely recognized features of postmodernism, what is often spoken of as the "hermeneutics of suspicion."

30. Butler, *Postmodernism*, 50–51.
31. Foucault, *Power/Knowledge*, 117.

Literary texts are not seen as artistic products existing in a rarefied realm of beauty and truth, nor as moral guides, nor as expressions of a writer's deepest feelings. Rather, literary texts (and other artistic products) are politically motivated and have political aspirations. Whether the writer knows it or not, she is promoting the interests of some power as soon as she sits down to write. Ideology unconsciously shapes a text, setting boundaries and determining what is permitted into the text and what is excluded. As a result, no naive reading of "what's there" suffices:

> The concepts which are excluded (absences, lacunae), and the problems which are not posed adequately (semi-silences, lapses), or not posed at all (silences), are therefore as much a part of the problematic as are the concepts and problems that are present. And it cannot for that reason be grasped by a simply literal or immediate reading of the explicit discourse of a text. Rather it must be reached by a "symptomatic" reading where the explicit discourse is read conjointly with the absences, lacunae and silences which, constituting a second "silent discourse," are so many symptoms of the unconscious problematic buried in the text. Like all knowledge, reading, correctly understood and correctly practiced, is not vision but theoretical labour and production.[32]

When Marx is fused with Freud, as he is in many postmodern thinkers, the reasons for suspecting the surface of the text increase exponentially. Texts betray not only various forms of latent political content but also latent psychosexual content. The reader's, and especially the critic's, goal is to scrape back

---

32. Quoted from Norman Geras in David McLellan, *Marxism after Marx* (Boston: Houghton Mifflin, 1979), 299. The quotation is describing the theory of Louis Althusser.

the surface of the text and expose the political and psycholog-
ical machinery beneath.

Not only texts but truth itself is an effect of power. Foucault,
fond of making play with the Baconian connection of power and
knowledge, argues that all regimes of power are also regimes
of truth. What counts as truth is not determined by the merits
of argument or evidence but by the power constraints at work
in a particular society. Each society, Foucault claims, "has its
regime of truth, its 'general politics' of truth," which determines which discourses are accepted and function as true. The
regime of truth involves not only a reigning "worldview" but
also the institutions and practices that filter claims and classify
them as true or false. By organizing human beings and human
institutions, furthermore, power creates a field of study, a field
of knowledge. People are spatially organized, and this makes
possible the reduction of human activities to "tabular form."
As Foucault says, problems of classification, of the "table," are
critical to eighteenth and nineteenth-century science, politics,
and other areas of study.[33]

Postcolonial and Postmodern

Marxist and Marxo-Freudian patterns of thought tell only
part of the story, however. As we have seen, postmodern
political theory arises as much from late-twentieth-century
events as from nineteenth- and twentieth-century theories. Postmodernism is a postcolonial project that aims to give voice
to the voiceless, to the marginalized of Western societies and
those cultures marginalized by global economic powers. It is
no accident that Derrida was doubly marginal—first as a Jew,

33. Foucault, *Discipline and Punish*, 186–87.

second because he was African (Algerian) by birth. Flagrantly homosexual, Foucault likewise is a voice from the margins.

Again, this effort to give voice to the voiceless affects the details of textual interpretation. Derrida is interested not only in what appears on the pages of the texts he reads but also in what fails to appear, in the silences and white spaces. As exercises of power, discourses necessarily exclude; saying *this* means not saying *that*.

This same aspiration lies behind the postmodern hostility to totality and totalizing grand narratives. Postmoderns see a terrifying symmetry between modern theories, which suppress inconvenient facts, and modern colonial conquest, which suppresses inconvenient peoples. Any grand scheme of history necessarily leaves things out and places some hero at the center of the story. In a totalizing scheme, history becomes the story of the increasing self-consciousness of Spirit, or of class conflict leading toward consummation in a classless society, or of the spread of democratic capitalism until we have achieved the end of history. But a story of the spread of democratic capitalism leaves out the tyrannical and socialist. Postmodernists want to bring those excluded stories into the center.

Revisions of the Western "canon" of great books arise from the same impulse toward justice. The canon is formed, the argument goes, not merely on the basis of objective criteria of literary quality but also on a political basis, to serve the needs of the dominant classes of Western societies and ensure their own hegemony in following generation. A canon that includes Homer and not Sappho, Aquinas but not Averröes, Faulkner but not Chinua Achebe contains an implicit hierarchy of male over female, Christian over Muslim, white over black. Those who have been left out of the canon deserve to have a voice.

In short, postmodern notions of power are fundamental to postmodern notions of the text and of the self. There is more than a little irony in this situation. After all, totalizing stances toward life, such as Islam and fundamentalist Christianity, are among the most popular options in the very postcolonial portions of the world that postmodernists aim to rescue from oblivion. Perhaps it's worse than irony: perhaps the postmodernist thinkers who claim to speak for the oppressed themselves harbor hidden class, race, and geographic prejudices. After all, the notion that metanarratives are in decline makes most sense to highly placed secular intellectual elites in Europe and America.[34] Perhaps postmodern theory is the ideology of rich and well-fed members of the knowledge class. Pointedly: Faced with the conservative Anglican archbishop of Nigeria, Peter Akinola, what do postmodern liberators have to say? That he's an Uncle Tom?

Solomon among the Postmoderns?

Solomon would not have been surprised to learn that power pervades human relations, or that oppression is common, or that genuine knowledge is subjugated and forgotten, or that rulers rule by surveillance. Though a king of only a small principality in the eastern Mediterranean, Solomon had pretty much seen it all. He had married Pharaoh's daughter, and his ships traded across the sea. He would stand with the postmoderns in unmasking the impossible pretensions of modern politics. If all is vapor, *of course* it is impossible to keep religion and politics, public and private, us and them, then and now neatly confined in their separate compartments. The vapor will seep

34. This observation is made pointedly by Butler, *Postmodernism*, 14–15.

out, mingle and mix and get confused. Modern political life, he would recognize, is a massive and massively doomed effort to shepherd wind. The Hebrew word for "wind" (*ru'ach*) also means "spirit," and Solomon knew that human beings, animated by spirit, are beyond human shepherding.

He also knew that "in the place of justice there is wickedness and in the place of righteousness there is wickedness" (3:16). Power often belongs to ruthless oppressors, who leave the oppressed with no comforter:

> I looked again at all the acts of oppression which were being done under the sun. And behold I saw the tears of the oppressed and that they had no one to comfort them; and on the side of their oppressors was power, but they had no one to comfort them. (4:1)

So common is the reality of unrelieved oppression that Solomon "congratulated the dead who were already dead more than the living who are still living" (4:2). But the unborn are even more blessed, because they have "never seen the evil activity that is done under the sun" (4:3). Oppression of the poor and the failure of justice is so common that we should "not be shocked at the sight" (5:8).

Foucault's talk of surveillance would have not surprised Solomon: "for one official watches over another official, and there are higher officials over them" (5:8).[35] And Solomon knew well enough that people gain a hearing and sometimes notoriety not because of their wisdom but because of their social position. A rich man who speaks folly is more likely to be heard than a poor man who speaks wisdom. And even if the poor man is heard, he will not long be remembered:

35. The translation and interpretation of this passage are notoriously difficult, but I'm taking the NASB translation straightforwardly.

> There was a small city with few men in it and a great king came
> to it, surrounded it and constructed large siegeworks against it.
> But there was found in it a poor wise man and he delivered the
> city by his wisdom. Yet no one remembered that poor man. So
> I said, "Wisdom is better than strength." But the wisdom of the
> poor man is despised and his words are not heeded. (9:14–16)

It is a classic case of "subjugated knowledge," knowledge ignored because it came from the margins, because it came from
them and not from *us*.

Yet Solomon sees all this without falling into Foucault's
Nietzschean despair and pessimism. And the reason is the same
reason we have been discovering throughout our exploration:
Solomon's unblinking examination of power and oppression
is pervaded by an eschatological faith that this world of tears
under the sun is not the only world, a confidence that there is
a time after the time under the sun. He knows that oppression
and injustice often flourish, but he is confident that they will
not flourish forever. He knows that under the sun there is no
perfect justice or final judgment, but he also looks to the time
when "God will judge both the righteous man and the wicked
man" (3:17), when God will "bring you to judgment for all
these things" (11:9). He finishes his book, fittingly enough, with
a declaration of faith in eschatological judgment. Oppressors
might hide themselves in their Panoptical fortresses; persecutors
might fill the earth with the blood of the innocent; dominant
classes might interpellate to create subjected subjects. But in
the end, "God will bring every act to judgment, everything that
is hidden, whether it is good or evil" (12:14).

5

Eat, Drink, Rejoice

I said in the introduction that I wanted to offer a "stance" rather than an "agenda," and I'm sticking with that plan. The stance is simple to describe: it is the stance Solomon recommends in Ecclesiastes, a stance of faith, joy, and worship. In the midst of postmodern mist and vapor, Christians are called to be Christians.

Faith first: Solomon emphasizes the vaporousness of human achievement, the elusiveness of the world and the self, the limits of our knowledge, with all the rhetorical power of the most nihilistic postmodern theorist. He agrees with postmoderns that the modern project was always doomed and was never entirely what its PR department said it was. He knows there are no absolute differences between *us* and *them*, that human control of the world is always partial, that the freedom that results from our control is always limited, that this windy world will not stay put in the little labeled file boxes we make for it. Solomon seems content, for a time, to stand among the postmoderns.

But he speaks the language of postmodernism not, finally, to affirm it; not, finally, because the vapor is all there is. Solomon talks like a postmodern to emphasize that the world is built to force us to live by faith and not by sight. This too is something of a postmodern move. Moderns aspired to live without faith. They could see nearly everything, and anything they couldn't see either was not worth seeing or would come clearly into view in short order. But they didn't see everything, and the best of them knew it. Postmoderns know that they can't see everything and that they can't see anything with perfect clarity. Some postmoderns have turned toward traditional Christian faith, but others, still haunted by modern aspirations and failures, conclude that if we can't have perfect clarity we'll stop playing the game altogether.

"Vapor" pictures the world as impossible to control. But vapor is also a veil, a screen. Think of how hard it is to drive through a thick fog. Everything disappears. You know there's still a world and a road out there, but the vapor keeps them hidden away. To say that all is vapor is to say that it's hiding something, and Solomon is suggesting that the vapor of the world screens us from God himself, who for the time being, "under the sun," modestly remains behind the veil of the vaporous world.

We don't yet see God putting everything right. We don't see the sovereign hand of poetic justice. Innocents die, sages are ignored, moral pygmies rule the airwaves and the movie screens and many nations. That's what it's like to live in a world of vapor. And that's just what we should expect once we wake from our modern Promethean nap and realize we are creatures, made from dust, living in a world made from nothing at all. On what were we drunk when we began to imagine we could figure it all out?

As I've emphasized throughout this little book, Solomon directs attention specifically to the eschatological dimension of biblical faith, and here he radically parts company with postmodernity. In directing our hope to a God who will emerge from the mist to judge the world in righteousness, Solomon ultimately places before postmoderns a series of fundamental choices, a Kierkegaardian Either/Or: to live, like Derrida, with the frustrating nihilism of eternal *differance or* to live with faith that there is a God concealed in the midst of the vapor; to lurch toward a messiahless noneschaton *or* to live in hope that God will bring all into judgment; to accept that injustices will never be righted *or* to trust a God who will judge every person according to what she or he has done; to give up all hope that the wind can be shepherded *or* to trust the One Shepherd who rides the wings of the storm (Eccles. 12:11).

And faith means joy: if some have read Ecclesiastes as the bitter reflections of an aging impotent cynic, others have read it as a hedonistic tract. Solomon regularly punctuates his meditations with exhortations to enjoy life: "There is nothing better for a man than to eat and drink and tell himself that his labor is good" (2:24–25). Again, "I know that there is nothing better for them than to rejoice and to do good in one's lifetime; moreover, that every man who eats and drinks sees good in all his labor—it is the gift of God" (3:12–14). What is good and fitting? "To eat, to drink and enjoy oneself in all one's labor in which he toils under the sun during the few years of his life which God has given him; for this is his reward" (5:18).

Modernity has for many moderns been a singularly joyless place. Weber's portrait of modernity as a stiflingly rationalized and technological "iron cage" is one-sided, but it expresses a common experience of modernity. And no wonder: if the burden of reducing the world to order fell on you; if you were tasked to construct a theory of *everything* and then write out the equation; if you had to be on constant patrol along the empty razor-wired borders between religion and politics, art and life, theology and philosophy, nature and society, us and them; if you had to ensure that the trinity of control, freedom, and progress remained in place for the ages—if you had all this to do, you might not exactly be bubbling buoyantly with childish glee.

By unmasking the pretenses of modernity, postmodernity has freed us from the burden of controlling reality. What a relief— except that most postmoderns immediately undermine our relief by saying that *nobody* is in control. That's why postmoderns can be as gloomy a bunch as moderns. But Solomon shows a way to real joy: the realization that we're not in charge, we never were in charge, and we don't need to be in charge, because that's Someone Else's job. For Solomon, the life of faith is a life of joy because faith liberates us from the burden of taking care of a creation that was never ours to begin with. Like a later sage, Solomon encourages us to be as children, and he opens the gate to the playground, where we eat and drink under the loving gaze of our Father.

And worship: Solomon not only wrote Ecclesiastes but built a temple in Jerusalem. The temple doesn't make an obvious appearance in Ecclesiastes, but it's there in Solomon's exhortations to "eat, drink, and rejoice." The only place in the Torah where these three verbs appear together is in Deuteronomy 14, where Moses instructs Israel to pay tithes at the sanctuary, where they are also commanded to celebrate before Yahweh: "You may spend the money for whatever your heart desires: for oxen, or sheep, or wine, or strong drink, or whatever your heart desires; and there you shall eat in the presence of the LORD your God and rejoice, you and your household" (Deut. 14:26). When Solomon exhorts us to eat, drink, and enjoy life, he is, like Moses, calling us to worship. As Jeff Meyers puts it, Ecclesiastes is not just about the mist; it's about a table in the mist.

The psalmist Asaph was troubled by the injustices of the world, and particularly by the puzzling prosperity of the wicked, "until I came into the sanctuary of God" (Ps. 73:17). In worship, we participate in the age to come—the world after the world under the sun—and in this moment of encounter with the God hidden in the mist, we glimpse something of a pattern in the vapor. And we can say with Asaph, "But as for me, the nearness of God is my good; I have made the Lord GOD my refuge, that I may tell of all Your works" (Ps. 73:28). Or, with Solomon, "There is nothing good for a man under the sun except to eat and to drink and to be merry, and this will stand by him in his toils throughout the days of his life which God has given him under the sun" (Eccles. 8:15).

Index